Creating CDS and DVDs

Tom Bunzel

Contents

3 Using Media Player to Enjoy CDs and DVDs 84

4 Capturing Video and Images with Easy Media Creator 106

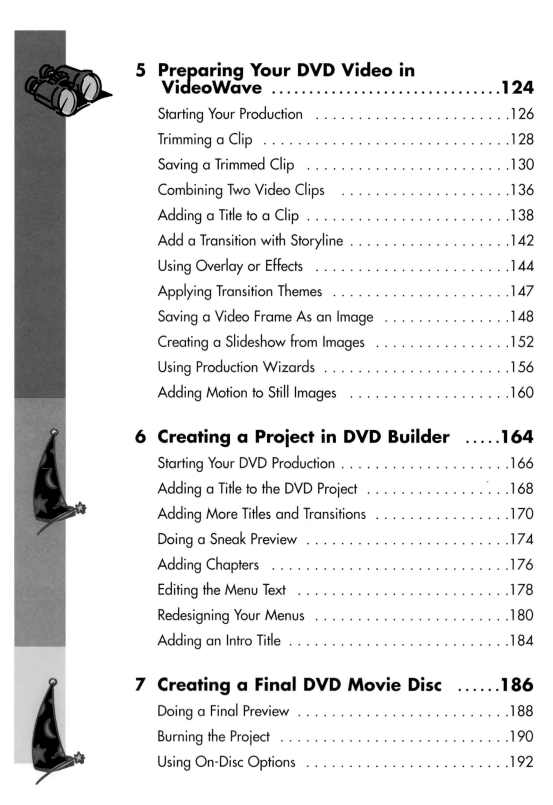

Easy Creating CDs and DVDs
Copyright © 2005 by Que Publishing

International Standard Book Number: 0-7897-3345-5

Library of Congress Catalog Card Number: 2005922645

Printed in the United States of America

First Printing: May 2005

08   07   06   05   4   3   2   1

Trademarks

All terms mentioned in this book that are known to be trademarks or service marks have been appropriately capitalized. Que Publishing cannot attest to the accuracy of this information. Use of a term in this book should not be regarded as affecting the validity of any trademark or service mark.

Warning and Disclaimer

Bulk Sales

Que Publishing offers excellent discounts on this book when ordered in quantity for bulk purchases or special sales. For more information, please contact

U.S. Corporate and Government Sales

1-800-382-3419

corpsales@pearsontechgroup.com

For sales outside of the U.S., please contact

International Sales

international@pearsoned.com

Associate Publisher
Greg Wiegand

Acquisitions Editor
Michelle Newcomb

Development Editor
Laura Norman

Managing Editor
Charlotte Clapp

Project Editor
Dan Knott

Production Editor
Benjamin Berg

Indexer
Chris Barrick

Technical Editor
Greg Perry

Publishing Coordinator
Sharry Lee Gregory

Multimedia Developer
Dan Scherf

Designer
Anne Jones

About the Author

Tom Bunzel is a technology coach, giving one-on-one instruction in PowerPoint and presentation skills. He works with well-known speakers and educators on their presentations, and specializes in multimedia and rich media production.

As Professor PowerPoint, Bunzel has appeared on TechTV's "Call for Help," providing PowerPoint tips and tricks on national television. Bunzel's most recent book is *Easy Digital Music*. His other titles include *Sams Teach Yourself PowerPoint 2003 in 24 Hours* and *How to Use Ulead DVD Workshop* (Que Publishing), as well as *Digital Video on the PC* (Micro Publishing Press).

Dedication

In loving memory of my mother, father, and Alan Shapero.

Acknowledgments

Thanks to Margot Maley Hutchison, for all of her help and support. My gratitude also to Michelle Newcomb, Laura Norman, Greg Perry, and the rest of the folks at Que.

We Want to Hear from You!

As the reader of this book, *you* are our most important critic and commentator. We value your opinion and want to know what we're doing right, what we could do better, what areas you'd like to see us publish in, and any other words of wisdom you're willing to pass our way.

As an associate publisher for Que Publishing, I welcome your comments. You can email or write me directly to let me know what you did or didn't like about this book—as well as what we can do to make our books better.

Please note that I cannot help you with technical problems related to the topic of this book. We do have a User Services group, however, where I will forward specific technical questions related to the book.

When you write, please be sure to include this book's title and author as well as your name, email address, and phone number. I will carefully review your comments and share them with the author and editors who worked on the book.

Email: feedback@quepublishing.com

Mail: Greg Wiegand
          Associate Publisher
          Que Publishing
          800 East 96th Street
          Indianapolis, IN 46240 USA

For more information about this book or another Que Publishing title, visit our website at www.quepublishing.com. Type the ISBN (excluding hyphens) or the title of a book in the Search field to find the page you're looking for.

1 Each step is fully illustrated to show you how it looks onscreen.

It's as Easy as 1-2-3

Each part of this book is made up of a series of short, instructional lessons, designed to help you understand basic information that you need to get the most out of your computer hardware and software.

2 Each task includes a series of quick, easy steps designed to guide you through the procedure.

3 Items that you select or click in menus, dialog boxes, tabs, and windows are shown in **bold**.

Drag

Drop

How to Drag:
Point to the starting place or object. Hold down the mouse button (right or left per instructions), move the mouse to the new location, then release the button.

24

Combining Audio Tracks

Start

PART 1

Ctrl+ Click

Click

Right-Click

1 **Ctrl+click** to select two (or more) tracks that you want to merge.

2 **Right-click** on the selected tracks.

3 Select **Merge Tracks**.

4 The merged track now exists in the project *in addition to the original two tracks, with the transitions cleared.*

End

INTRODUCTION If you like, you can combine more than one track into a single song for your audio CD. For example, this technique is helpful if you have a favorite sequence of dance tracks that you want to merge into a single track for your audio CD project.

TIP **Splitting Tracks** To split up merged tracks, just right-click the merged tracks, and select **Split Tracks**. Obviously you can now add transitions between them if you like.

HINT **Merge Narration with Songs** If you've imported a track with narration, you can merge it with a song to introduce it in your own personal way, such as "dedicated to," and so on.

Introductions explain what you will learn in each task, and **Tips and Hints** give you a heads-up for any extra information you may need while working through the task.

See next page

See next page:
If you see this symbol, it means the task you're working on continues on the next page.

End

End Task:
Task is complete.

Selection:
Highlights the area onscreen discussed in the step or task.

Click:
Click the left mouse button once.

Double-click:
Click the left mouse button twice in rapid succession.

Right-click:
Click the right mouse button once.

Pointer Arrow:
Highlights an item on the screen you need to point to or focus on in the step or task.

Click & Type:
Click once where indicated and begin typing to enter your text or data.

Introduction

The Magic of CDs and DVDs

If you've been in a computer store or an audio or stereo dealer lately, you've noticed a "convergence" of products. The same media or discs that hold the data for the computer also store movies and music in the world of consumer electronics.

So it's no surprise that consumers want to be able to create or "burn" their own audio and data CDs and DVDs as well as movie DVDs.

Accomplishing this task in the Windows world involves two major programs: Nero 6 Ultra Edition and Easy Media Creator 7 (formerly from Roxio but now distributed by Sonic Solutions).

Both of these programs allow you to complete the main tasks involved with burning CDs:

- Ripping music from an audio CD
- Storing music in various formats
- Burning a personal music collection to your own audio CDs
- Backing up your most important files on a data CD or DVD

So we'll cover these tasks in both suites of programs—Easy Media Creator 7 and Nero Ultra.

But audio is only part of what most people want to do. You've got pictures and video that you want to use to create DVD projects with movies and slide shows.

Sonic Solutions's Easy Media Creator has greatly enhanced its ability to expand on just creating audio and data CDs. From working with audio, it's just a short jump to creating background music for slideshows, working with video, and putting our video onto a movie DVD.

Where we once needed other programs for these tasks, we'll be able to continue to work in the Easy Media Creator suite. After burning audio CDs, we'll capture video into the Sonic Solutions's Capture program and edit in VideoWave.

VideoWave will also let us assemble a slide show of our favorite images. In some of these VideoWave projects we'll be able to edit our video footage and integrate the audio we used earlier into the soundtrack.

Our next step in the Easy Media Creator suite takes us to DVD Builder, where we'll add our video and slide shows as titles, create chapters in our longer clips, and create an interactive menu that lets a user navigate through the project. Then, just as we burned audio and data CDs and DVDs in Creator Classic, we'll be able to burn a true movie DVD right out of DVD Builder.

If you're a Nero Ultra user, you can follow many of the same concepts and create a DVD movie disc using the features in the Nero suite, even though we don't get specifically into that application for these tasks.

Along the way we try to do what the salesmen in the stereo and computer stores seldom are able to accomplish—we're going to break down the tasks into simple steps and we're going *anticipate and answer the most common problems and address the most significant issues* by bringing them to your attention before you trip over them yourselves.

Remember that both of these *suites of programs* have the tools you need to create your own digital discs for music, data, or DVD movies. Using them effectively is only a turn of the page away.

Creating CDs with Creator Classic in Easy Media Creator

So you've got a stack of audio CDs with your favorite artists and songs and you'd like to do a few different things:

- Get the music from your audio CDs into your PC.
- Store folders of your favorite music on your PC in the best possible formats.
- Organize, move, and burn other discs from your music collection and data files.

All of the tools you'll need are the within different programs in the Easy Media Creator suite. In this chapter we're going to concentrate on those tasks that involve creating music and data CDs, so the *application* we'll be using in Easy Media Creator is Creator Classic—Roxio's program for creating audio and data CDs and DVDs. Creator Classic saves the work you do as *project*. This means that each time you move songs from an audio CD, assemble them into folders, or burn a set of files to disc, you can save your set of choices by clicking File, Save, or Save As to save the project under a new name.

As you'll see, the names of the projects begin to accumulate at the bottom of the Easy Media Creator Home Page so that you can reopen the project file and continue working in any project right where you left off.

Creator Classic lets you save the music that you "rip" from your audio CDs in different computer file formats (such as WMA and WAV), in addition to compressing the files (in MP3 format) if you need to conserve space or to move them to a portable device. We'll discuss these various formats and how they're used most effectively.

By understanding how to work with PC music files, you'll also learn how to create archives of all your computer files that you can use to safeguard your most important data as a backup.

Eventually we'll also learn to use your audio projects and files in other applications, as we create videos in VideoWave and assemble a DVD project in DVD Builder.

Easy Media Creator provides many different ways to work with digital media.

Use the audio tasks to work with music

Use data tasks to work with computer files

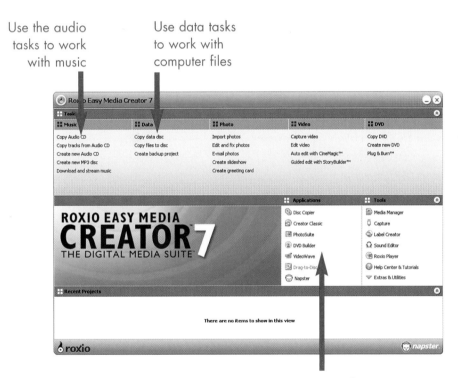

Launch an application to perform various tasks.

Getting Started with Easy Media Creator 7

Start

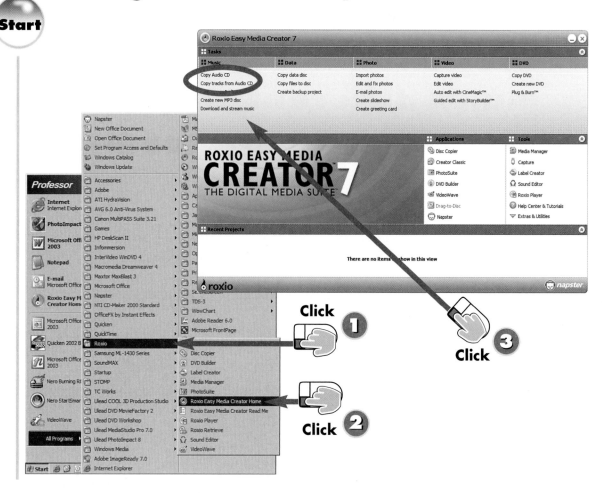

Click ①

Click ③

Click ②

① Click **All Programs, Roxio**.

② Click **Roxio Easy Media Creator Home**.

③ Review the various music tasks in the upper left. Click **Copy tracks from audio CD**.

The main menu for Easy Media Creator 7 is called the *home page*. From there, you can begin the task of creating your own music collection by "ripping" the tracks from an audio CD.

TIP

Use the Desktop Shortcut
You can also click the Roxio shortcut on the desktop to launch Easy Media Creator.

HINT

What Is Ripping?
The songs on an audio CD are stored in a digital format that most PCs can't understand. To work with them efficiently they need to be "sucked" from the disc and converted into a PC-friendly computer file format. This process is known as *ripping* an audio CD.

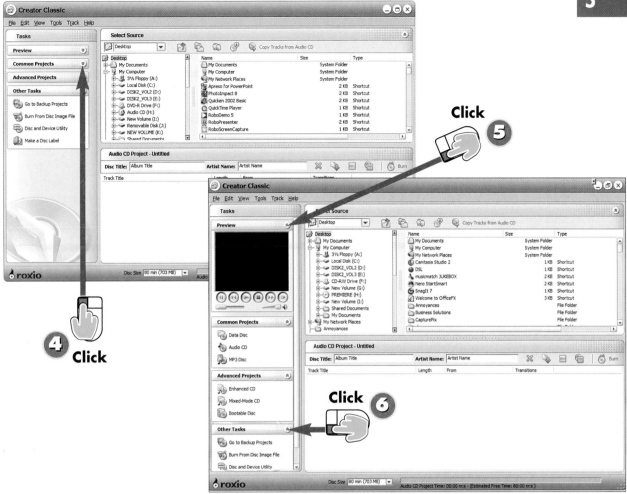

4 CD Creator Classic opens in an **audio CD project** to let you extract (rip) tracks from one or more audio CDs. Click the drop-down double arrow to expand the **Common Projects** window.

5 Click the drop-down double arrow to open the **Preview** window if it's not already open.

6 Click the drop-down double arrow to open the **Other Tasks** menu (if it's not already open) and review the other options available in Creator Classic.

End

Shortcut for Classic
TIP Creator Classic is *not* in the Roxio group in the Start Menu by default, but an icon for Creator Classic should be installed on the desktop. Or open it from the Roxio Home Page.

Set Screen Resolution
TIP Easy Media Creator 7 requires a screen resolution of at least 1024×768. Right-click on your Windows desktop, and select Properties. In the Settings tab, drag the Screen Resolution slider to 1024×768.

Preview Window
HINT The Preview window can be used to preview video files for a DVD or Video CD project.

Beginning an Audio CD Project with Creator Classic

Start

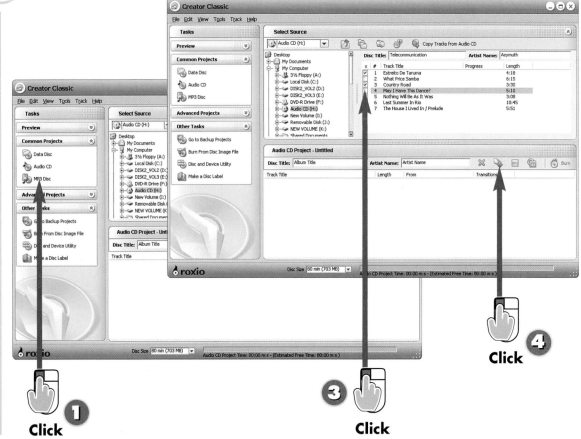

Click ① **Click** ③ **Click** ④

① Click the **audio CD icon** in the Select Source panel.

② Your album with all of the tracks selected appears in the Source panel on the right.

③ **Uncheck the tracks** you *do not* want to rip or extract.

④ Click **Add selected files above to project**.

INTRODUCTION

Since audio CDs are already in a digital format, you can extract (or "rip") music files from a disc using Creator Classic. First insert your audio CD into your CD or DVD recordable drive. While you can download music online or get it from other sources, your favorite songs in the best quality are probably on audio CDs.

TIP

How the Tracks Get Named Roxio accesses an online database of music to try to locate the title and track names of the audio CD you are using. You must have an active Internet connection for this to work. If the songs are not identified, we'll soon see how to name them manually.

HINT

Other Music Sources Eventually as you save your music to other formats, you'll see how to use those formats, like MP3, to assemble your own audio CD. This will enable you to combine tracks you download with tracks you rip from audio CDs.

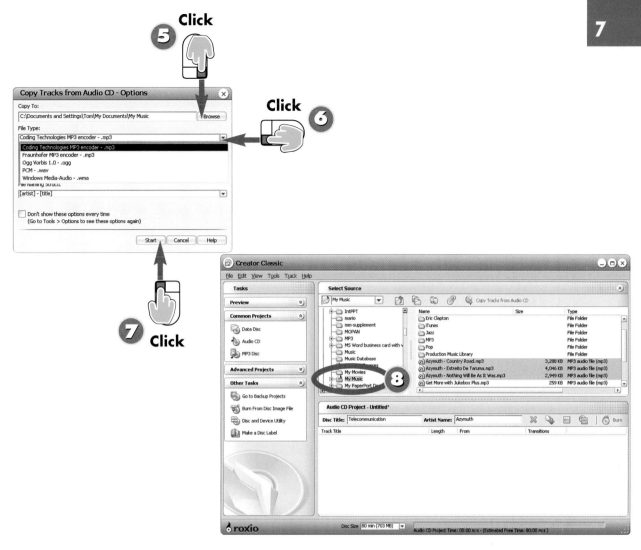

Click 5

Click 6

7 **Click**

8

⑤ Your files will be saved to My Documents\My Music by default. If you want the files saved to another location (not recommended for a beginner), click the **Browse** button.

⑥ Click the **File Type** down arrow to reveal the list of different file types (besides MP3) that you can use. For now, stick with WAV.

⑦ Click **Start** to begin the extraction of selected tracks.

⑧ Back in the Select Source window, click the **My Music** folder within **My Documents** to view the songs that have been extracted in the format you chose.

End

Catch the WAVE
Remember that choosing MP3 compresses the tracks. To save your cuts as true CD quality audio, you would select the **WAVE (.WAV)** file format from the drop-down list.

Preview Your Tracks
You can preview a track on the audio CD before you decide whether to copy it to a file or burn it. Click to select or high-light it, and then click **Track, Play** on the Main Menu in Creator Classic.

Transferring Audio Files to CD

Start

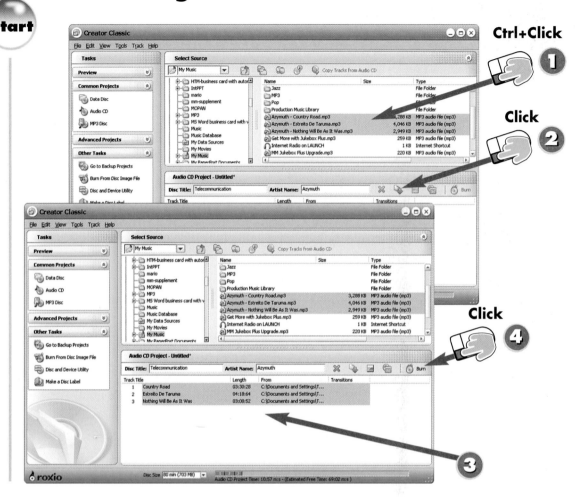

Ctrl+Click **1**

Click **2**

Click **4**

1 **Ctrl+Click** to select the music files in the My Music Folder that you want to burn to a new audio CD.

2 Click the **Add to CD** audio project button.

3 The selected tracks are added to the audio CD project.

4 Put a blank CD into your recording drive and click **Burn** to begin recording the tracks in CD audio format.

Now that you've saved the sound files on your computer, by accessing the My Music folder, you can add them (and other ripped or downloaded audio tracks) to any audio CD project.

Using Different File Types
As we'll see when we assemble a music library, downloaded MP3 files can be combined with extracted .WAV audio files to burn a new audio CD.

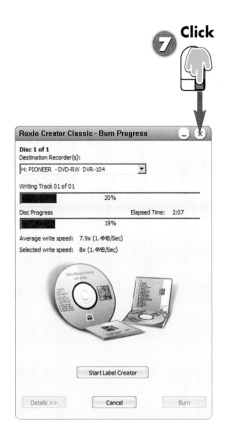

Click 7

Click 6

5 Confirm that the drive that has the blank CD for burning is listed as the **Destination Device**.

6 Click **Burn**.

7 Watch the disc burn to completion and then click the **Close (X)** button to close the window.

End

What You've Burned
HINT
If you've saved your files in MP3 format rather than .WAV, you've actually burned CD audio tracks with compressed audio files. Due to the compression, it won't be true CD quality. But, because of the small size, MP3 is the preferred file format for music downloads.

Burning a True MP3 Disc
TIP
If you prefer to maximize disc space and use MP3 format tracks, you can choose to burn an MP3 disc under Common Projects. Newer audio CD and DVD players will play MP3 discs, and we'll cover them in another chapter.

Saving Audio CD Tracks As Computer Files

Start

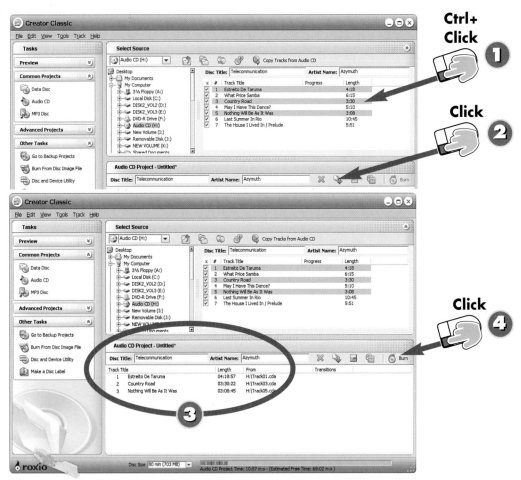

Ctrl+
Click

Click

Click

1 **Ctrl+click** to select individual tracks you want in your audio CD.

2 With the tracks selected (highlighted), click **Add selected files above to project**.

3 The tracks are added directly to the audio CD project.

4 Click **Burn** to record the audio CD directly (without saving the tracks to your computer).

Let's do a similar audio CD project, but this time we'll store the files on your PC in the highest possible quality as computer files you can reuse over and over again. Insert your favorite audio CD and let's give it a try.

HINT

Why Save Your Tracks?
If you keep your music as files on your computer you won't always be looking for the disc to play a particular song, or to burn a new compilation of your favorite tunes for a special event or other occasion.

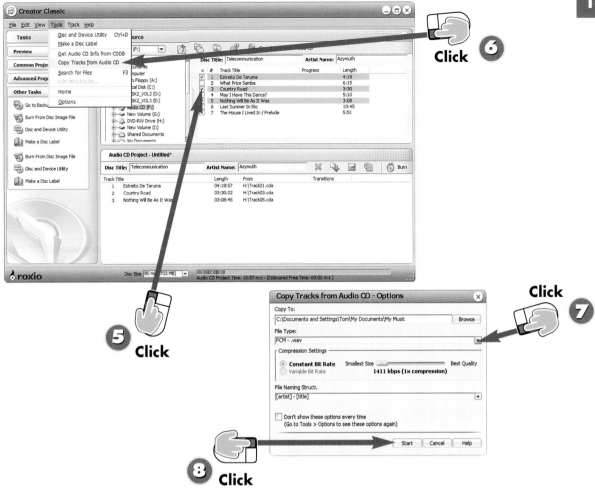

5 Click to **uncheck** (deselect) any files you don't want saved to your computer.

6 Click **Tools**, **Copy Tracks from Audio CD**.

7 Click the **File Type** drop-down list to select the PCM WAV format.

8 Click **Start**.

End

What You Just Did
The first set of files seen in the audio CD project had *.CDA file extensions—they were true unconverted CD audio tracks as they appear on the source CD. When you saved the tracks as WAV files, the quality was preserved and you can find them in the My Music folder as *.WAV files.

Saving Your CD Audio Project
If you think you want to return to your CD audio project, save it (File, Save) before beginning a new project. Remember that if you want to go directly from other audio discs, and not computer files, you will need those discs to continue or change the project.

Creating a Music Library

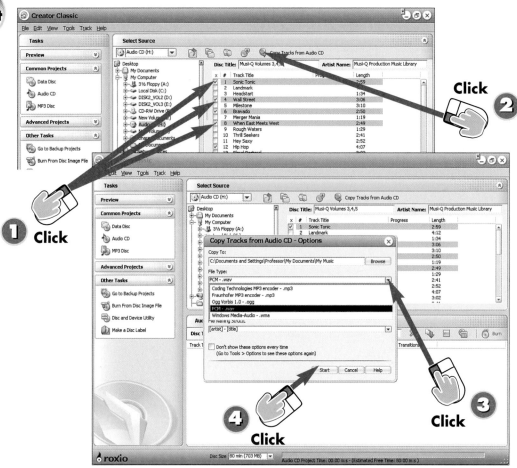

In an audio CD project, click to **deselect** (uncheck) the songs you *don't* want added to your computer library.

Click **Copy Tracks from Audio CD**.

Click the **File Type** drop-down arrow to select the file type you want the songs saved with.

Click **Start**.

In Easy Media Creator 7, you can maintain a library of your favorite songs to play or burn in different combinations in other projects. Depending upon your hard drive capacity or taste in music quality, you may want to save your files as *.WAV, *.MP3, or perhaps as highly compressed *.WMA files.

Selecting Copy Tracks File Types
Use .WAV files if you have plenty of hard drive space and want the best possible music, and also don't care about moving the songs to a portable device. Use .MP3 files to combine compilations with downloaded songs, preserve hard drive space, and move the files to portable players. Use .WMA files to use up the least hard drive space and to move files to the smallest portable music players. Check the software with your music player to determine the type of file format that will work best on the device.

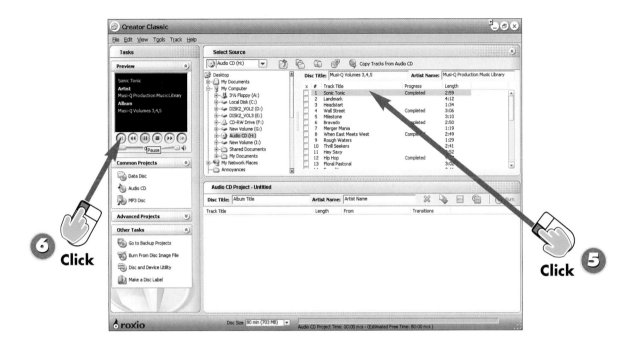

End

The tracks you left checked are converted into the file format you selected, in the folder you chose. Click a completed song to view its information in the preview window and begin to hear a preview.

Click **Pause** or click to select and preview the other completed songs.

Choosing Tracks
Clicking tracks in the Select Source window enables you to play (listen) and preview them. This lets you decide which ones to check and uncheck in the boxes next to the tracks to decide which ones are saved to the local folders when you click Start.

Making Destination Music Folders

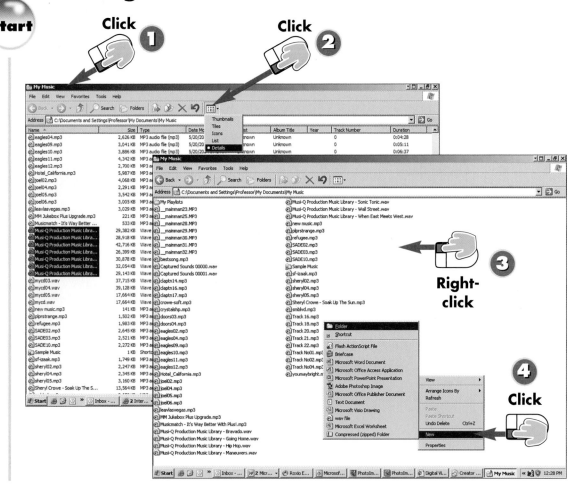

1. Click **My Documents** on the Start Menu and open the folder (the default is My Music) to which you copied your WAV or other song files from the audio CD.

2. Click the **View** drop-down arrow and select **Details** to be able to see the saved files and their file sizes.

3. Right-click in a blank part of the window to bring up the submenu.

4. In the submenu, click to select **New**, **Folder**.

Detailed View

HINT

Changing to Detail view in the My Music folder will not affect the view of other folders in Windows. If you open another folder, the view will default to icon view, or whatever you've set as your default view.

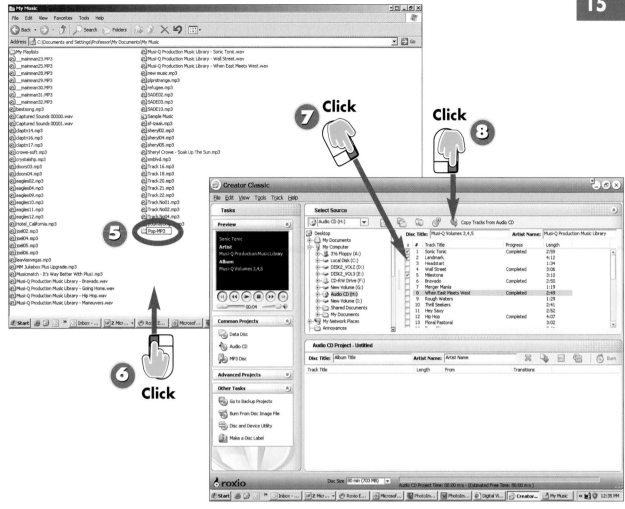

5 Type a name for the new folder. You can name it for the file type you want to save your music files in, or use the name of a type of music.

6 Click elsewhere in the folder to set the folder name.

7 In Creator Classic, check (or uncheck to deselect) songs to save in another format.

8 Click **Copy Tracks from Audio CD**.

See next page

Getting on Track
You may have to reinsert the same audio CD to get all tracks checked for you—or simply (re)check the tracks you want to save again in a different format or location.

The Rename Game
You can also select a file or folder name by single-clicking on the name twice—like a slow double-click—or right-clicking it and choosing **Rename**. The name will be highlighted and you can type over it with a new name.

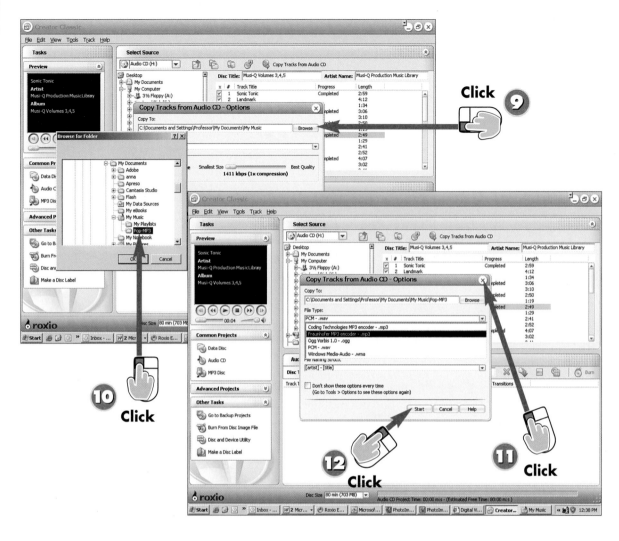

9 Click **Browse** in the Copy Tracks dialog box to locate your newly created folder.

10 Click to select the folder and click **OK**.

11 In the **Copy Tracks** dialog box, select a different file type in which to save the songs to this location (like ***.MP3**).

12 Click **Start** to begin saving these files to the newly created folder in the format you want.

INTRODUCTION

There are a lot of reasons why you should create a folder or set of folders for saving your projects and audio files. When you get into creating data CDs, you'll want to have folders just for those projects as well so that you can easily locate the right project and continue adding to the project, or burn the files to CD.

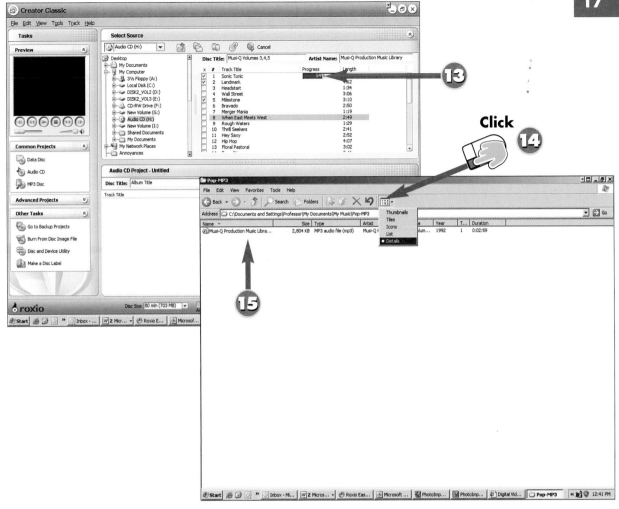

13 Watch as your songs are converted into the other format and saved to your new folder.

14 Click the **drop-down arrow** and select **Details** to view the file sizes and date modified of your new file(s).

15 Note the difference in file size from the files you saved as *.WAV files.

End

TIP

Get Organized
Once you've created your new folders, you can also drag and drop or copy and paste your other files into them to reorganize your music library.

Creating an MP3 Audio CD

Start

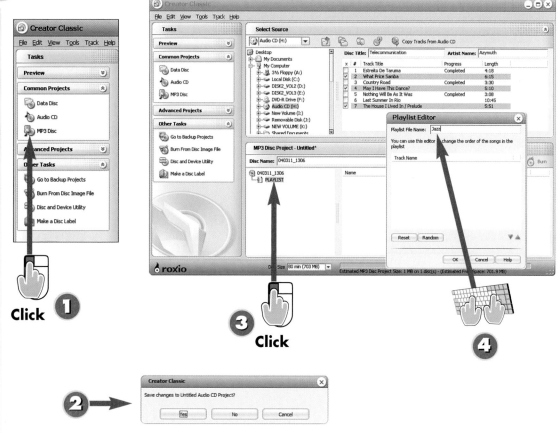

Click **1**

Click **3**

4

2 →

Creator Classic

Save changes to Untitled Audio CD Project?

Yes   No   Cancel

1 Click **MP3 Disc** in the Common Projects menu.

2 Determine whether or not you want to save or discard an existing audio CD project from the dialog box.

3 Click **Playlist** in the MP3 Disc Project window at the bottom of the screen.

4 Type a name for the Playlist, like **Jazz**.

INTRODUCTION

Once you've saved files in the.MP3 file format, Easy Media Creator 7 will also let you create an MP3 audio disc from the same project, which will play in many newer audio CD and DVD players.

TIP

File Name Length
Even though some audio CD players claim to play MP3 discs, they may not recognize tracks with overly long file names. You can adjust for this by going back into the Playlist. You can rename these tracks before you burn the MP3 disc by selecting them and pressing **F2**, or right-clicking and choosing **Rename**.

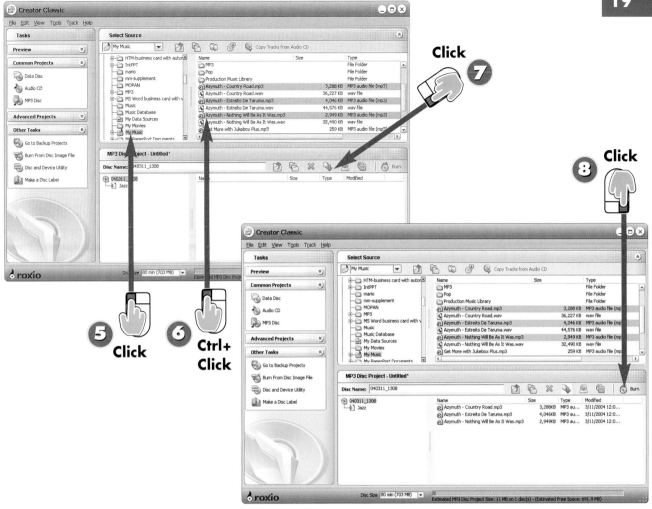

5 Click the **My Music** folder in the Select Source window (or wherever you saved your MP3 tracks).

6 Ctrl+click the names of the MP3 files to add to the disc.

7 Click **Add selected tracks above to project**.

8 Click **Burn** to begin recording the MP3 disc.

End

Changing Play Order
With the project set for your MP3 files, you can always reopen the Playlist and change the order of the tracks before you burn them.

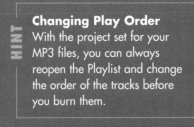

Adding Track Transitions to an Audio CD

Start Click

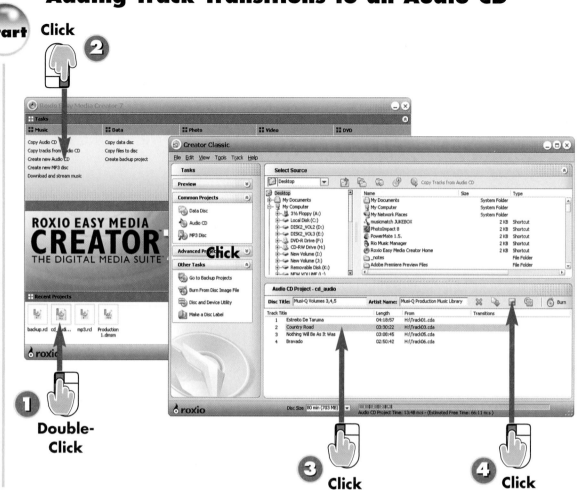

Double-Click

Click

Click

1. From the Roxio home page, double-click to an existing audio CD project listed in the Recent Projects window.

2. Optionally, you can click **Create new Audio CD** to start a new project from scratch (see previous tasks in this chapter to find out how to add music files to your project).

3. With your tracks added to the project, click one of the tracks to select it.

4. Click **Edit Track Transitions**.

INTRODUCTION

Previously in this chapter we used Creator Classic to create an audio CD. One way to enhance an audio CD is by putting transitions between the tracks, such as fading out of one track and into another. You can add transitions to an existing project or create a new audio CD project with track transitions.

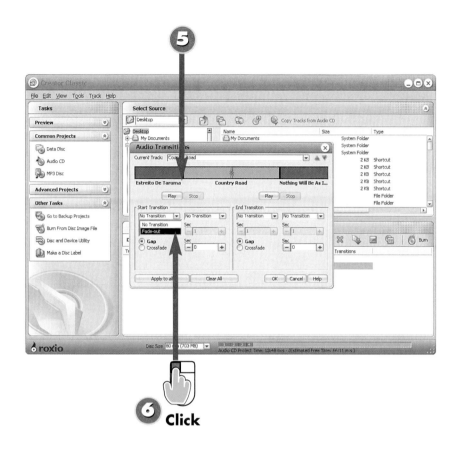

Click

5. Look at the selected track highlighted in the **Audio Transitions** panel, along with the previous and next track.

6. Click the drop-down list in the **Start Transition** box and choose **Fade Out**. The track prior to the one selected (in step 3) will now fade into the track that you selected.

See next page

Trouble with Transitions
If you plan on playing your audio CD on older CD players, be aware that transitions, and particularly longer gaps between tracks, can cause playback problems.

Test Your Transitions
Use the **Play** button in the Audio Transitions panel to play or preview the transitions you create.

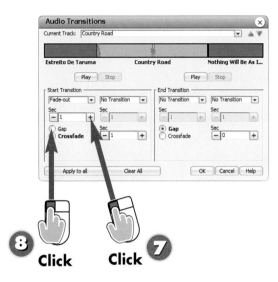

7 To increase the time between the end of one song and the start of the next, click the + sign for the **Gap** for as many seconds as you want the interval to last.

8 Repeat steps 6 and 7 in the **End Transition** box to add transitions with gaps or crossfades between the end of the selected track and the track that follows it.

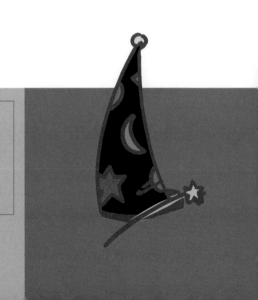

TIP

Using Crossfade
To make the interval represent the period where one song fades directly into the other, click **Crossfade** (deselecting Gap).

Click

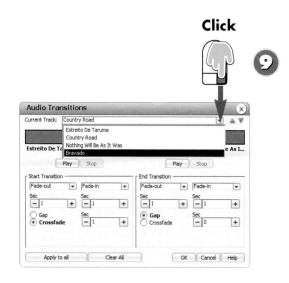

9

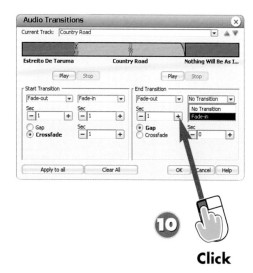

10

Click

9 Use the **Current Track** drop-down list to select another track to apply transitions to.

10 Repeat the process in steps 6–9 for the newly selected track.

11 Click **OK** when you're done to exit the transitions panel.

End

HINT

Checking Transitions
Icons representing the transitions you added are visible in the Audio CD Project panel under the Transitions tab after you close the Audio Transitions dialog box.

TIP

Quick Transitions
Click **Apply to All** to quickly apply the transitions for the current track to the entire CD.

HINT

Reopening a Transition
Click the transition icon next to any track if you want to change or remove its transition. Use the **Clear** button in the Audio Transitions panel to clear your transitions.

Combining Audio Tracks

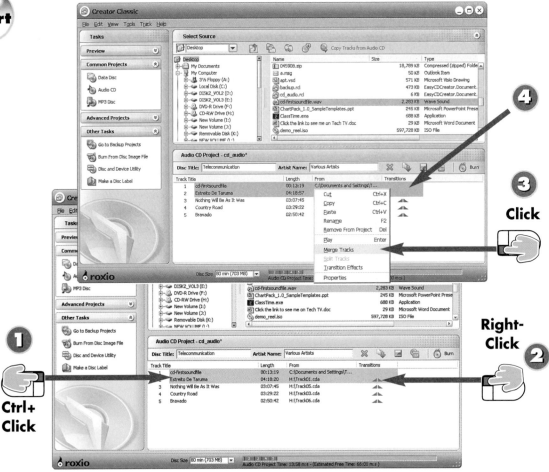

Ctrl+ Click

Click

Right- Click

1 **Ctrl+click** to select two (or more) tracks that you want to merge.

2 **Right-click** on the selected tracks.

3 Select **Merge Tracks**.

4 The merged track now exists in the project *in addition to the original two tracks*, with the transitions cleared.

End

Creating an Image File

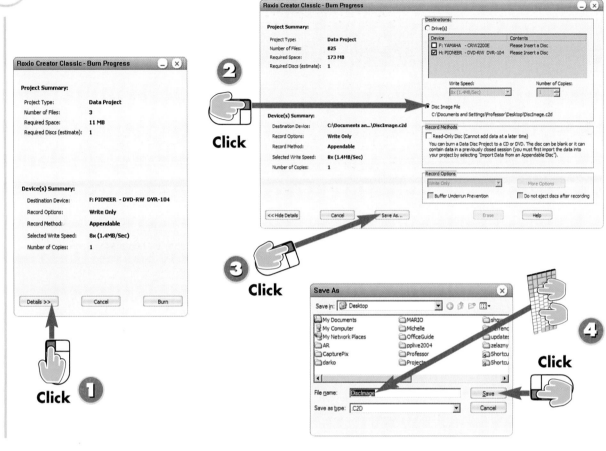

(1) After you click **Burn** in the Project panel, the Burn Progress dialog opens. Click **Details** to expand the Burn Progress dialog.

(2) Click the radio button to select **Disc Image File** for output.

(3) Click **Save As** to determine where to save the file and name it.

(4) **Type** a name for the image file and click **Save**.

End

With a compilation of CD-quality audio, MP3, or data tracks in the Project window, you can save a *disc image file* to burn additional discs of the same project at a later date. Not having to re-create your project to burn the same disc will save you time and steps.

TIP

Burn Progress Details
In the Burn Progress Details dialog, you can make other adjustments to your recording, including selecting an alternate CD or DVD burner if you have more than one in your system.

HINT

Image File Sizes
Use caution when creating a disc image. A disc image file can be *very large* because a CD holds up to 800 megabytes of data, and a DVD holds 4.7 *gigabytes* of data, which is converted into a single image file that is saved to your hard drive.

Burning an Image File to Disc

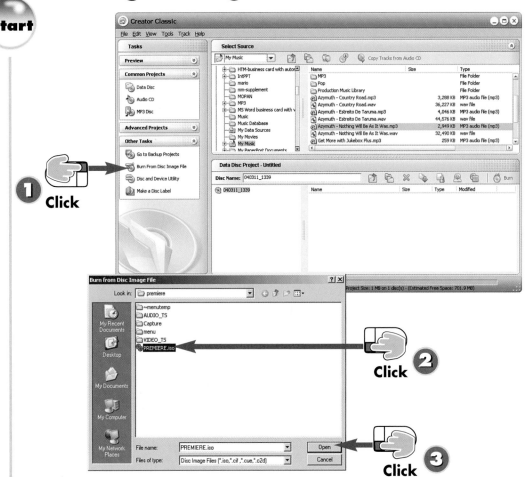

Start

1 Click

2 Click

3 Click

---

1 Click **Burn From Disc Image File** in Creator Classic's Other Tasks list.

2 Locate the image file (in *.ISO format) and click to select it.

3 Click **Open**.

With an image file of your project saved on your computer, you can open it any time and quickly burn it to a disc.

TIP

Using Image Files for Data?
Using image files for data backup is not very helpful because many of the files will be outdated by the time you burn the image file again. Keep a Creator Classic project file for data backups instead. The file is smaller and the program will tell if you if it's missing any component files.

TIP

Using Image Files Effectively
Image files are great if you want exactly the same content on a disc, which is probably most true for music compilations and perhaps picture slide shows or DVDs (which we will get to in the later chapters).

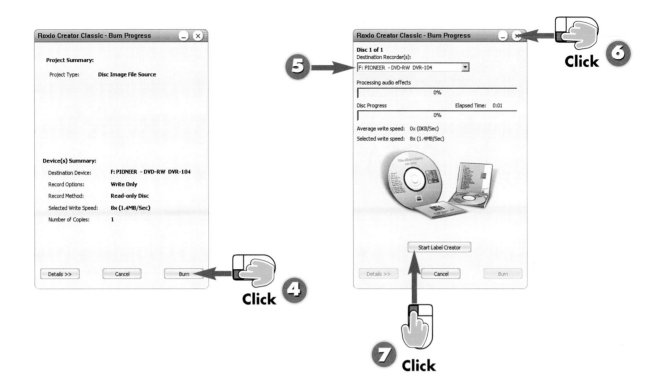

(4) Click **Burn** in the Burn Progress window.

(5) Confirm that the right recorder (CD burner) is selected. If not, click the drop-down list to select the right destination.

(6) Click **Close** to close the window when you're done.

(7) Optionally, click **Start Label Creator** and refer to the task "Making Your Own Disc Label or Insert" at the end of this chapter.

End

Saving Time

HINT

If you have a slow CD or DVD burner, you can burn a disc image during the day, which won't take as long as burning a disc, and then burn the disc from the image when you have more time.

Backing Up Image Files

HINT

Since image files get really big, you might consider using a data DVD disc to back up your favorite CD disc images. You could fit about six entire CD disc images (650 megabytes) onto one DVD disc (4.7 gigabytes).

Copying an Audio CD

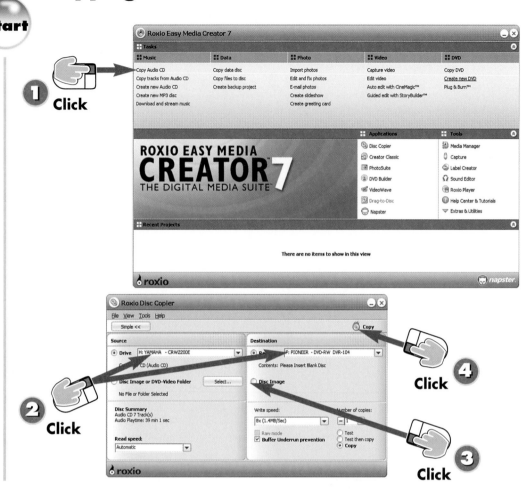

1. Click **Copy Audio CD** in the Music column of the Tasks window.

2. **Select** your source and destination CD or DVD burner.

3. If you have one recorder, select to create **a Disc Image**.

4. Click **Copy**.

End

INTRODUCTION

Copying is a task that you begin directly from the Easy Media Creator Home Page or by launching the Disc Copier application.

TIP

Copying a Data Disc
To begin copying a data CD from the Roxio Home Page, click **Copy data disc** under the Data menu, or launch the Disc Copier application.

TIP

Troubleshooting
If you have problems going from one recorder (CD or DVD burner) directly to another, either reverse the source and destination drives or create an image file first.

Continuing an Existing CD Project

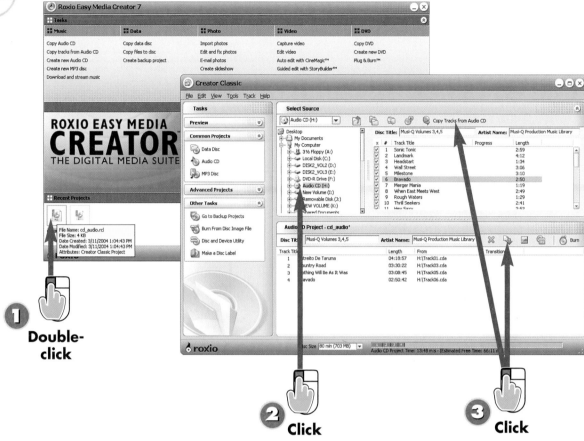

1 Double-click

2 Click

3 Click

1 Hover your mouse over the existing projects. Information related to the content of the project is shown as a reminder. Double-click a project icon to open Creator Classic and continue the project.

2 Click to select a drive with the additional audio CD tracks to add to your compilation or music file library.

3 Use the same techniques we learned previously in this chapter to copy tracks or add selected files to the project.

 End

INTRODUCTION

If you have saved your data, MP3, or audio CD project, it is easy to work with the same files and add more tracks in Easy Media Creator. To continue an audio CD project, put another audio CD into your CD or DVD recorder and look at the icons representing your saved *projects*, which appear in the lower panel of the Roxio Start Page.

HINT

Using Project Files
Project files aren't really files at all—they just point at or reference the files on an audio CD. Creating projects is a great way to save different compilations to reuse in the future without wasting hard drive space.

HINT

Saving Data CD Projects
You can also save your data CD projects to create further backups or file compilations (as we'll see in the next task), but it's important to make sure that you know that your files and folders are up to date and in the same location.

Making a Backup Data CD

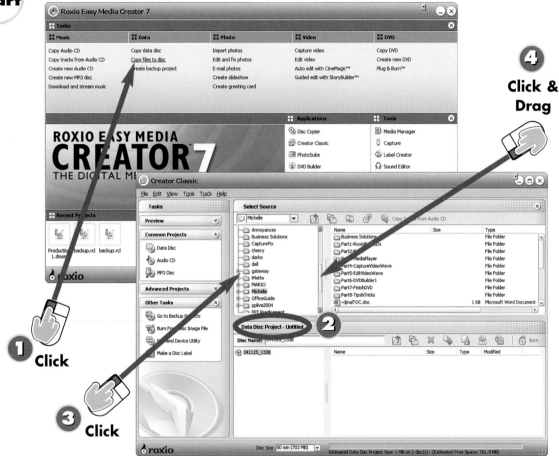

Start

4
**Click &
Drag**

1 Click

2

3 Click

---

1 On the Roxio Home Page click **Copy files to disc** in the Data column of the Tasks window.

2 Creator Classic opens with the familiar Windows file structure in a data CD project.

3 To reveal subfolders, click the **+** sign next to any main folder.

4 To locate more drives and folders, click and drag the scrollbar.

INTRODUCTION

Now that you've made music CDs, creating a data CD will be easy—it's just a compilation with *all kinds* of folders and computer files. When you insert a data CD or DVD in a computer, it will pop up in the My Computer window as a new drive and let you access the folders and files you burned.

TIP

Starting a New Data CD
If you're already in Creator Classic or open it as an application, you can always start a new data CD project by clicking the icon, or clicking **File**, **New Project**, **Data CD**.

HINT

Lifesaver
Burning and saving data CDs (or DVDs) is a great way to safeguard or back up your most valuable files.

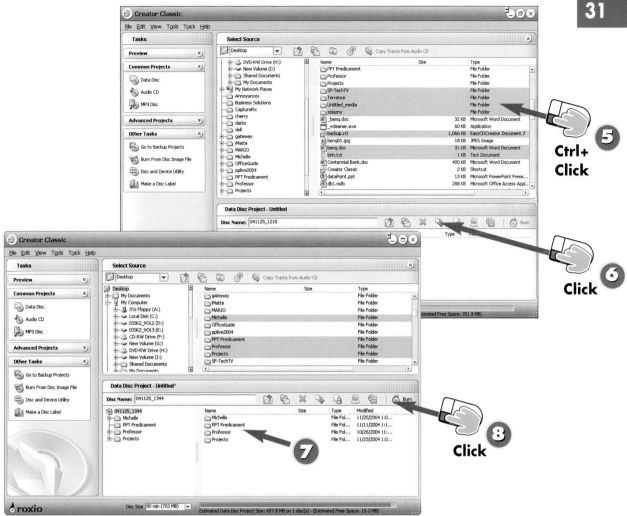

5 **Ctrl+click** to select multiple files and folders from the upper panel.

6 Click **Add selected files above to project**.

7 The bottom panel begins to fill up with the folders and files that will be burned to your data disc.

8 Click **Burn** to begin the recording process, just as you would with an audio CD.

End

TIP

Watch the Status Bar
The *status bar* shows how much data you will be able to fit on a CD (or DVD). Do not exceed capacity of your blank media. Remove files and folders by selecting and pressing the "X" (delete) button in the Project's window to decrease the amount of data you are burning.

HINT

Shortening File Names
If you see a dialog box requesting you to change or shorten the names of the files, go ahead and click **Change All**. This will increase disc compatibility with other computers.

Making a Backup Data DVD

Start

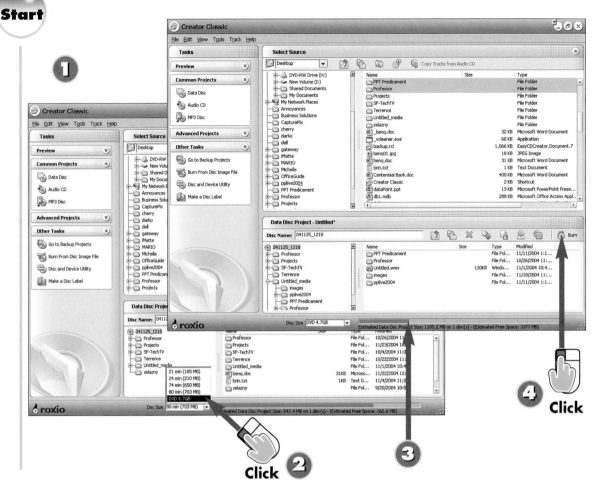

1 Put a recordable DVD disc into a DVD recorder in your PC.

2 Click the drop-down arrow on the **Disc Size** selector and select the DVD option.

3 As you continue to add more folders and files from the top panel to the bottom, notice your increased capacity.

4 When you've filled up the lower panel, click **Burn** to record your DVD disc.

Later in this book we will create the most commonly used DVDs, which are movie discs with interactive menus. But a blank DVD disc can also be used to store lots of data instead of showing movies, and unlike a blank CD, which typically holds about 700 megabytes of data, a blank recordable DVD disc holds 4.7 *gigabytes*.

Starting a Data DVD
If you're already in Creator Classic or open it as an application, you can always start a new Data DVD project by clicking the icon, or clicking **File**, **New Project**, **Data DVD**.

Be Smart and Safe
Burning and saving data DVDs (or CDs) is a great way to safeguard or back up lots of your most valuable files on one inexpensive disc.

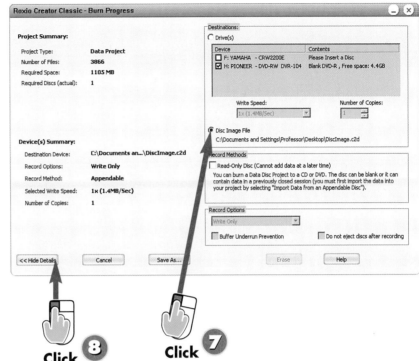

5 Click   **Click** **6**

Click **8**   **Click** **7**

5 To change recorders or choose other options click **Details**.

6 With the proper recorder chosen in the Destination Device field, click **Burn** again to begin recording.

7 Optionally, you can click to also record a **disc image file** to make more copies later.

8 Click **Hide Details** to return to the main Burn panel and begin recording the DVD.

End

Setting Options in Creator Classic

Start

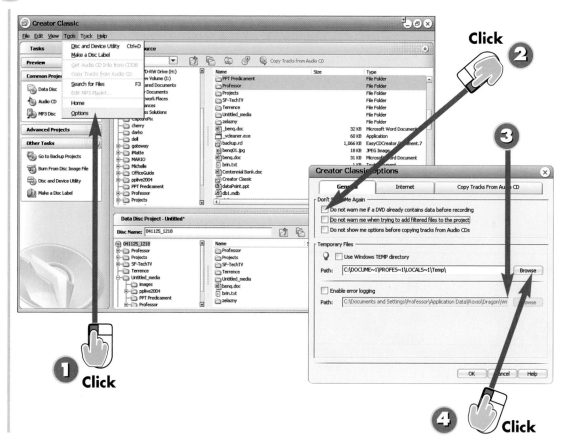

Click 2

3

Click 1

4 **Click**

1 Click **Tools**, **Options** in Creator Classic.

2 Click to deselect showing any warnings that may be slowing you down.

3 Notice the location for error logging files (to use for tech support).

4 Click **Browse** if you need or want to change the location of where your temporary files for disc burning are located.

TIP

Temporary Directory
Most of the defaults for these options are fine. However, if you get burn errors, make sure the temporary directory is on a disc with enough empty hard drive space to store one or more entire CD or DVD discs.

TIP

Create a TEMP Directory
Don't use the Windows TEMP directory for temporary files unless you only have one hard drive (the main C drive) and you know it has plenty of space.

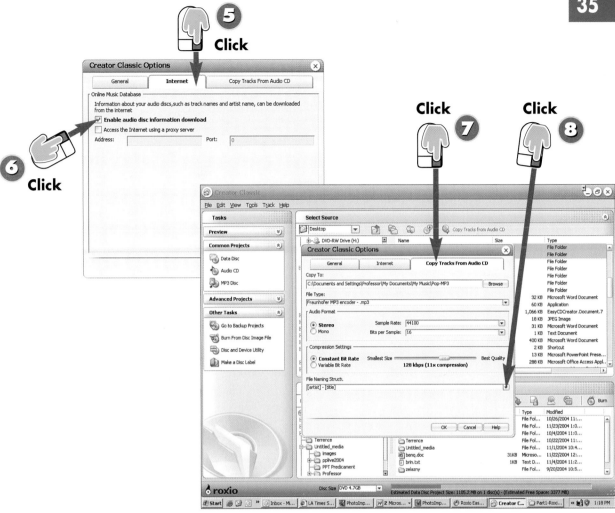

5 Click the **Internet tab**.

6 Make sure that you have checked **Enable audio disc information download** to add the disc information to your ripped CDs.

7 Click the tab for **Copy tracks from audio CD**. Check or set new defaults in the appropriate fields to change where ripped files will be stored, and which formats you prefer.

8 Note or change (by clicking the drop-down list in the File Naming Struct field) the file naming structure that you prefer to help you organize your music files.

End

Stay Organized
Remember that you can alter the destination folders for ripped CD files before you extract them, but setting the folder options here will speed up that process and keep your files organized.

Automatic Naming
Checking **Enable disc information download** prompts Roxio to check its online database to fill in artist and track information automatically. This makes it easier to name your tracks when you transfer them as files to your PC.

Enhancing File Names
Click the drop-down choices under the **File Naming Struct** options to add items like album names to your file names in your music library.

Making Your Own Disc Label or Insert

Start

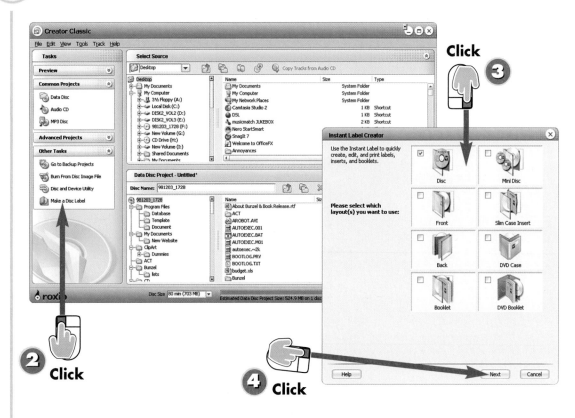

Click

③

Click

② Click

④ Click

---

① Reinsert the new disc you just burned.

② Click **Make a Disc Label** in Creator Classic.

③ Click the check box next to the type of label you want to make.

④ Click **Next**.

Once you've recorded a data or audio CD, you may want to create an adhesive cover for the disc or a label for the jewel case. You can use the Roxio Label Creator for this and open it directly from Creator Classic.

All Kinds of Labels
The same principles we're using here for a data disc label will also apply for an audio CD.

Plastic Applicator
Many label packets and kits will include a simple plastic applicator for making sure you put the adhesive label directly on the CD without folds or errors. These make the application process a snap.

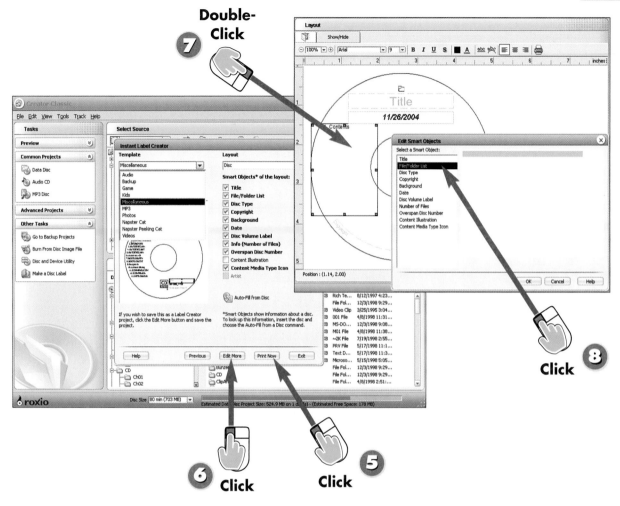

Double-Click **7**

Click **8**

Click **6** **Click** **5**

5 Once you've found a template and layout you like you could click **Print Now**.

6 To make more refinements to the label click **Edit More**.

7 Double-click the **Contents** Smart Object.

8 Select the **File/Folder List** object and click **OK**.

See next page

Opening Label Creator
You can also start Label Creator directly from the Roxio home page.

Accessing Smart Objects
The disc must be in the drive to access the Smart Objects to populate the label.

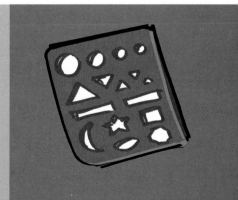

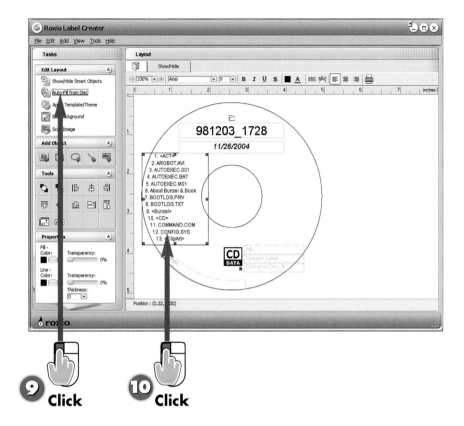

9 Click **Auto-Fill from Disc**.

10 The Smart Object is filled with the list of files and folders (or audio tracks) on the disc.

INTRODUCTION

There are many more refinements to the labels you can make like adding images and changing fonts and colors. Click **Help** to get more information on those features.

TIP

Files Appearing on the Label
Only the first group of files will appear on the label, depending on the size of the smart object. Resize it larger to hold more files or folders, or name the files or folders with an "_" as the first character to put them at the top of the list.

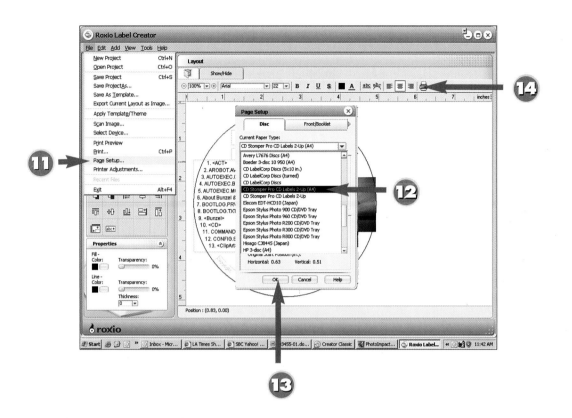

11 Click **File**, **Page Setup**.

12 Select the label or paper type.

13 Click **OK** to close Page Setup.

14 Click **Print** to print the labels.

End

Inserting Labels
Pay special attention to the way you need to insert the labels into your printer and read your printer documentation to make sure the labels are right for the printer.

Check Your Label Package
To find out which kind of label template or layout to use in the Label Creator, check the serial number and make and model of the label package you intend to print and find the closest match in the Page Setup panel.

Previewing the Label
You can click **File**, **Print Preview** to see how the individual label will look. To make even more certain it's going to print with no surprises, you can print a test label on plain paper first.

Burning CDs and DVDs with Nero 6 Ultra

Nero Burning ROM is one of the most popular digital disc production programs on the planet. Nero supports a true .CDA file format to recognize digital audio in its native format, so that it doesn't need to be converted or compressed to any PC file. And, it can also burn a true movie DVD (or VCD or SVCD), but we'll cover these formats with Easy Media Creator.

For now, we're going to concentrate on burning audio CDs of your favorite music and creating data CDs to safeguard your most precious files. You'll also learn to create combination discs and even print custom labels and sleeves.

There are a few ways to approach Nero. We're going to start with Smart Start, a common interface that is organized by tasks in an intuitive way that leads to the appropriate program in the Nero suite for the project.

There are two main versions of Nero: Nero Express for quick and simple burning and Nero Burning ROM for more detailed and precise compilations. In this part we'll work with both.

While we won't cover the rest of these programs, you may want to explore NeroVision Express as an alternative way to capture video, author DVDs, and create photo slide shows, using the same techniques we cover for Easy Media Creator 7.

The easiest way to get acquainted with Nero is by opening the Smart Start interface. There's an icon for it on your Start Menu or you can open **All Programs**, **Nero**, **Smart Start**.

Nero Has Many Applications

Use Applications to launch a
specific program

Use the Favorites
to begin a project

Create an audio CD (or
perform another task)

Beginning Nero with Smart Start

Start

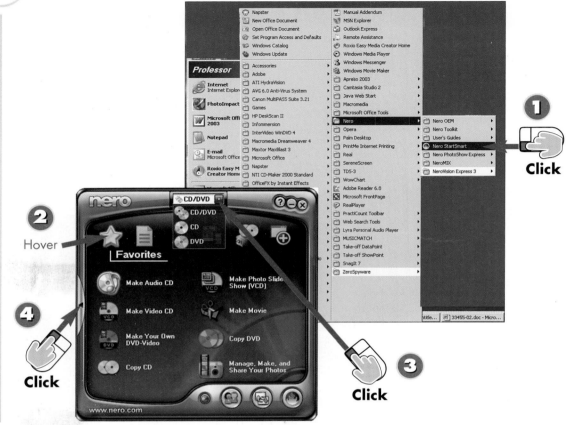

1 Open Nero Smart Start by clicking **Start**, then **All Programs**, **Nero**, **Smart Start**.

2 Hover over the various icons at the top of the Smart Start screen to see the six main types of tasks you can perform.

3 Click the drop-down arrow to select either a CD or DVD format, or leave the dual choice.

4 Click the **Show/Hide Applications bar** to give you more selections.

Smart Start is an interface organized by Nero's most commonly used tasks and provides access to Nero's other applications, tools, and manuals. By going through the Smart Start menu together, we'll get a great idea of what we can accomplish and the many tools Nero has at its disposal.

TIP

Nero Updates
Click the **Nero Product Center** icon on the lower right of the panel to go directly to the Nero website to download updates and newer versions of the product. It's a good idea to check this on a regular basis.

TIP

Access Nero Manuals
Click the **Manuals** icon to open a panel that lets you open PDF files to give you more help on the applications.

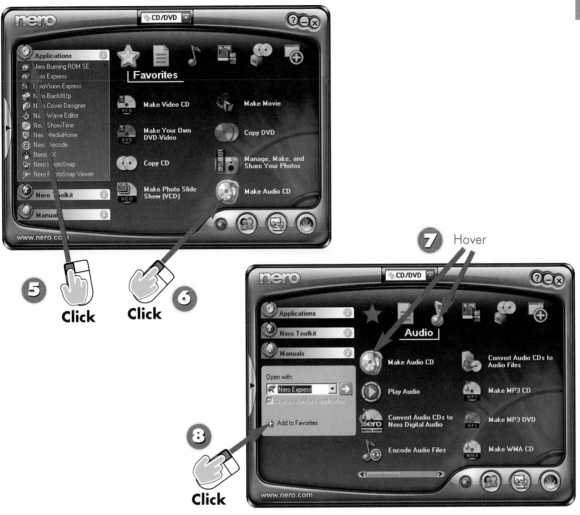

Click   Click   Hover   Click

5 Click **Applications** to reveal the different programs that come with Nero Ultra.

6 The tasks in Smart Start open the appropriate program, like **Make Audio CD** to launch Nero Burning ROM.

7 Hover over the **Audio** icon to see those specific tasks and then hover over the icon to **Make Audio CD**.

8 Click **Add to Favorites** if you want to have this task appear on the Favorites panel.

End

HINT
Customize It
You can use the buttons at the bottom right to change the appearance of Smart Start, restore program defaults, and toggle between standard (when you're new to the program) and expert (once you've got your feet wet).

TIP
Add Tasks to Favorites
Use the drop-down arrow above the Add to Favorites option to determine which application opens for a given task: Nero Express (which is the default) or Nero Burning ROM.

HINT
Use the Toolkit
Click the **Nero Toolkit** icon (below the Applications icon in the upper left of the screen) to open a panel that lets you check your hardware settings and burning capabilities.

Burning Your First Data CD with Nero Express

Start

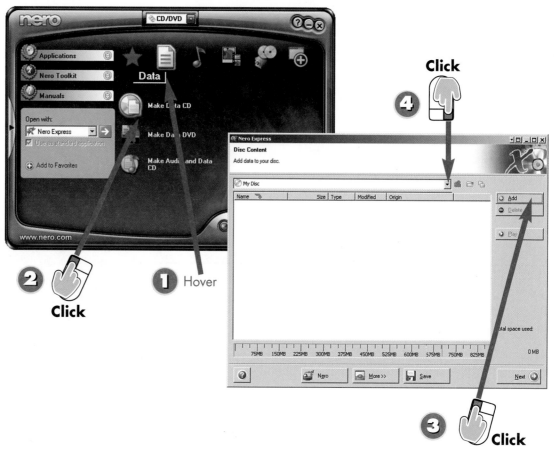

Click

1 Hover over the **Data** icon to activate the various data CD options.

2 Click **Make Data CD**.

3 Click **Add** to begin adding folders and files to the project.

4 The File Selector will open for Nero Express.

We'll use the Smart Start menu to create your first CD, which will be made up of files on your computer. This is a great way to back up important files, such as those on the Desktop or in the My Documents folder, and is a good introduction to burning any type of CD with Nero.

TIP

Take Advantage of Undo You can undo the addition of a set of files by pressing **Ctrl+Z** (or redo with Ctrl+Y).

TIP

Switch Between Programs When you hover over the choice Make Data CD, notice that the default choice is to use Nero Express. After you get more comfortable with the tools, you can still switch to Nero Burning ROM for the project by clicking **Nero**.

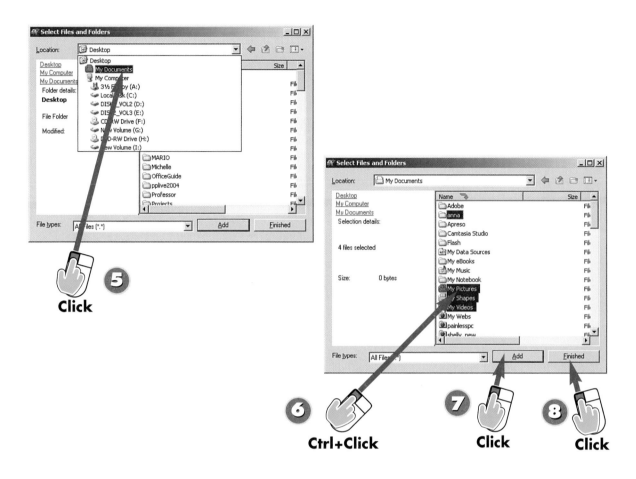

Click ⑤

⑥ **Ctrl+Click**   ⑦ **Click**   ⑧ **Click**

⑤ Select **My Documents** by clicking it.

⑥ Use **Ctrl+click** and/or Shift+click to select multiple folders or files in the **My Documents** folder.

⑦ Click **Add**.

⑧ When you've added enough folders and files, click **Finished**.

See next page

Selecting a DVD disc

TIP — The default disc type is CD. If you want to burn a DVD disc, change the media type to **DVD**.

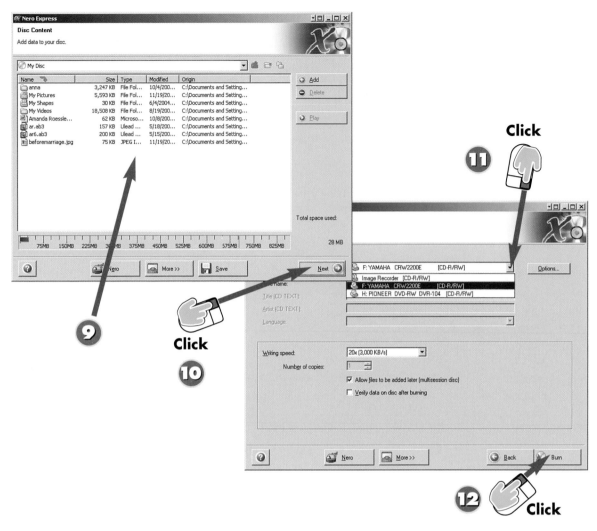

9 After you review the files, it's time to put a blank CD or DVD disc into your CD or DVD recorder.

10 Click **Next** to begin burning the disc.

11 Click the drop-down arrow to select a CD or DVD recorder if you have more than one.

12 Click **Burn**.

As you add data, you can keep track of the total size of the disc on the bottom status bar, to make sure that you don't exceed the capacity of your CD or DVD media. Note that if you drag a folder with subfolders, the folder structure is reproduced in the *root folder* of the CD.

Creating a Disc Image

TIP

If you want to save a file on your computer that you can burn over and over again, select **Image Recorder** as your destination. This creates an image file (in the *.NRG file format) and places it on your hard drive to burn again at a later date.

Use the Default Burn Speed

TIP

You can determine a burning speed or let Nero set the maximum speed. You should use the Nero default whenever possible, and just lower the burn speed if you encounter problems writing to your media.

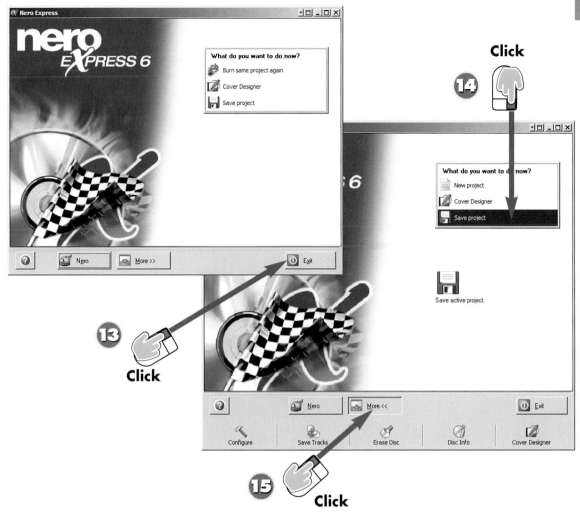

Click

Click

Click

13 When burn is complete click **Next** (not shown), then click **Exit** or continue in Nero Express.

14 Click **Save project** to save the project file so you can use it again.

15 Click **More** to see additional options for checking the system or the disc.

End

Using the Project File
Saving the project file lets you reopen the same referenced set of files again later. Reopen the project file the next time you begin Nero Express to continue working with the same files.

Starting an Audio CD with Nero Burning ROM

Start

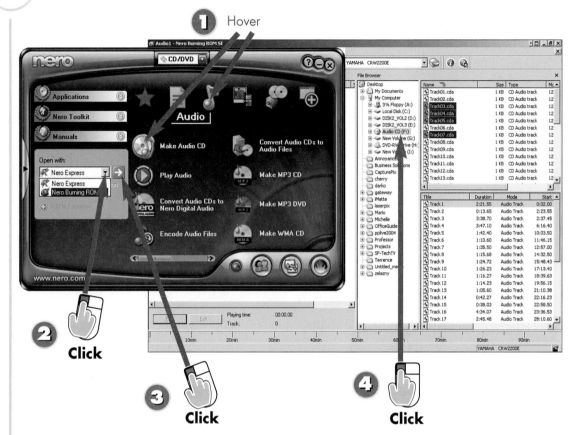

① Hover

② Click

③ Click

④ Click

① In Nero Smart Start, hover over **Audio** and then **Make Audio CD** until you see the drop-down menu that says **Open with**.

② Select **Nero Burning ROM** to make it your default music CD program.

③ Click the green arrow to launch Nero

④ Put an audio CD into your CD (or DVD) drive. Click on the CD drive letter in the File Browser and watch the tracks come up in the right panel.

HINT

Take No Action
Windows XP will sometimes pop up and prompt you for action when you insert a new CD of any kind. It's a good idea to select "take no action" when you're already in the middle of a project. We will discuss how to "train" Windows XP to make that the default action in the future.

Drop

Drag

Click

6

5

7

8 **Click**

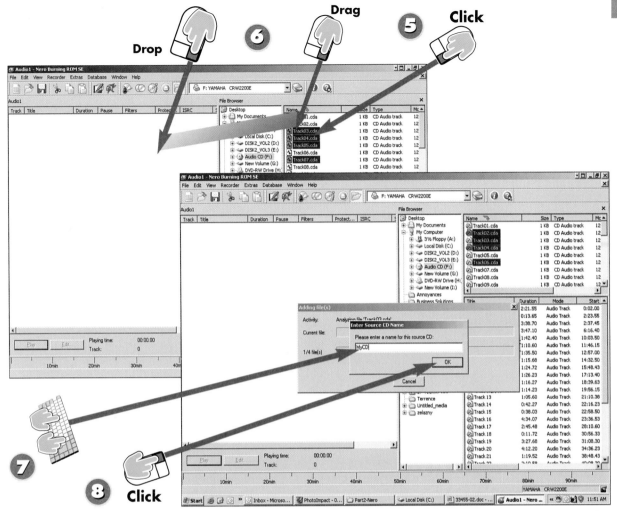

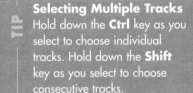

5 Click to select one or more tracks from the CD to include in the compilation.

6 Drag and drop them into the compilation panel on the left.

7 Enter a name for your CD project.

8 Click **OK** to begin extracting or "ripping" the files.

See
next
page

Selecting Multiple Tracks
Hold down the **Ctrl** key as you select to choose individual tracks. Hold down the **Shift** key as you select to choose consecutive tracks.

Previewing the Tracks
You can select the tracks in the compilation and click **Play** to listen to them to make sure they're the songs you want.

What's the Nero Database?
The Nero Database is a way of tracking and organizing your music, and naming saved files automatically. We will cover it later in this chapter. For now, if the window opens, just click **Cancel** to escape.

Adding file(s)

Activity: Analyzing file 'Track04.cda'...

Current file: ▮▮▮▮▮▮▮▮▮▮▮▮

2/4 file(s) ▮▮▮▮▮▮▮▮

Cancel

9 Watch

10

11

9 Watch as Nero rips or extracts the CD audio tracks.

10 Put a blank CD into your CD (or DVD) drive.

11 Click **Burn**.

INTRODUCTION

As you continue with your audio CD project, you'll see Nero copying the tracks from your audio CD and saving them on your computer—a process commonly known as *ripping*. In the remainder of this task you'll burn the tracks as soon as they're ripped, but in the next task you'll see how to maintain your extracted tracks as audio files on your computer, to play and reuse over and over again.

HINT

Check the Status Bar
Keep an eye on the bottom of the window to see how much time (space) you have left on the audio CD.

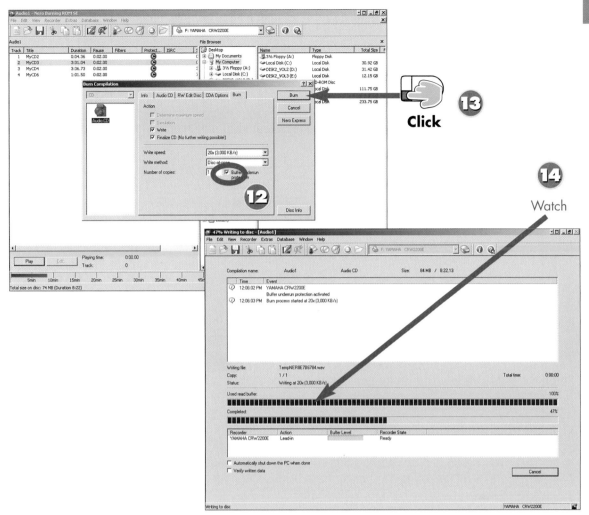

Click 13

Watch 14

12 Check to make sure **Buffer underrun protection** is enabled.

13 Click **Burn**.

14 Watch as Nero Burning ROM begins to burn your audio CD.

End

Refresh the Tracks
Whenever you reopen a formerly saved project file in Nero Burning ROM, click **File**, **Refresh Compilation**. Unless you've saved the tracks to your hard drive, you will need your original audio CDs.

Save Music Files
You've already created a data CD in Nero Express and you'll find that the process for burning an audio CD is very similar. The advantage of use Nero Burning ROM is the ability to save the audio CD tracks as *computer files,* as we'll see in the next task.

Use the Burn Defaults
The default writing speed and other defaults in the Burn Compilation window should work fine. We're going to explore them more thoroughly later.

Creating a Music Collection in Nero

Start

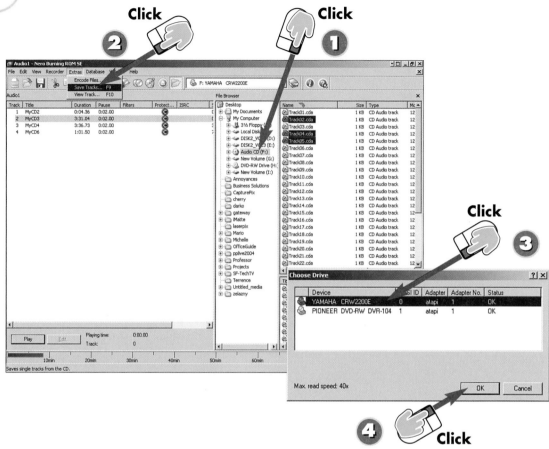

1. In Nero Burning ROM, put in an audio CD and click on the drive letter to access the tracks. If you need a reminder, see steps 1–4 in the previous task.

2. Click **Extras**, **Save Tracks** or press F8.

3. Confirm or select the recorder that has the audio CD with your music.

4. Click **OK**.

What if you want to keep your tracks available to play or to burn again in different combinations? You will need to save the audio tracks as *computer files* on your hard drive. Let's take a look at creating a personal music collection.

TIP

Cancel the Database Window
If the Database window pops up, click **Cancel** for now.

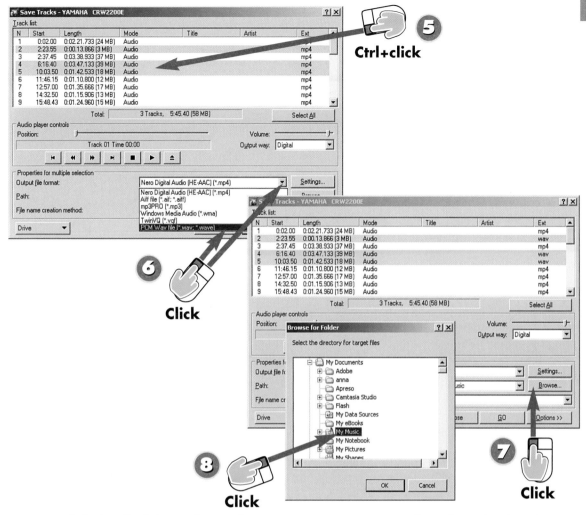

Ctrl+click

Click

Click

Click

By default, all of the audio tracks on your source CD are selected. To deselect them all, click elsewhere in the window, then **Ctrl+click** on one or more tracks to select the ones you want to work with.

Click the drop-down arrow in the **Output file format** field to choose WAV format.

Click **Browse** to select a new folder for the audio files (My Documents\My Music) or note the default destination.

Select a subfolder for music and click **OK**.

See next page

Accessing Your Tracks
You can continue with the old compilation or go through the steps of beginning a new audio CD project. You do not need to have tracks in the panel on the left—just source tracks in the panel on the right.

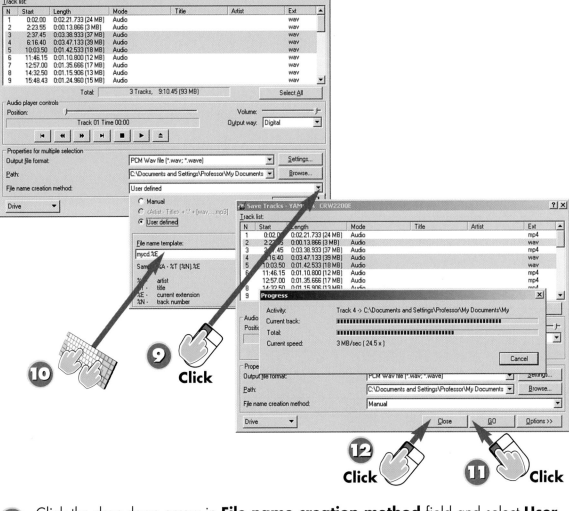

9 Click the drop-down arrow in **File name creation method** field and select **User defined**.

10 Type a name for the tracks like **MyCD** (or the name of the album or artist) and leave the ".%E" extension.

11 Click **GO**. You can watch the files being converted from CD audio to Windows WAV format.

12 Click **Close** to exit the **Save Tracks** dialog box.

By converting the audio CD files to a computer-friendly file format, you'll be able to use them in other applications. By naming and organizing them, you can enjoy your music in different combinations on the PC.

Why You Should Name Your Tracks

If you don't use the user defined option for naming the tracks, they will always be named just Track01, 02, and so on, and you will keep overwriting previously named tracks.

Automatic Naming for Tracks

To name the tracks automatically, see the task in this chapter called "Creating a Music Database in Nero," **p.66**.

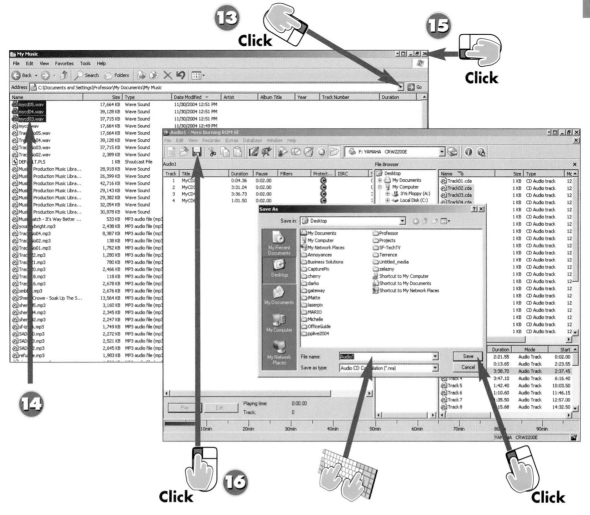

Click 13 15 **Click**

Click 16 **Click**

13 In Windows, open the **My Documents\My Music** folder, or whichever folder you chose to save your project to.

14 You should see your newly named and saved audio CD tracks saved as WAV files.

15 Click **X** to close the window for My Music.

16 Click the **Save the active compilation** button and save your project file. Name the project file and click **Save**.

 End

Encoded Files
Saving the files without compression as WAV maintains the best possible quality, but they are quite large. In another task we will *encode* them as MP3 files.

Saved Music Files
Once you've saved the files in WAV (or MP3 format, as we'll see in a subsequent task), they can be played from inside a Nero compilation, or using Windows Media Player or even RealPlayer for web music.

Burning Tracks from the Music Collection

Start

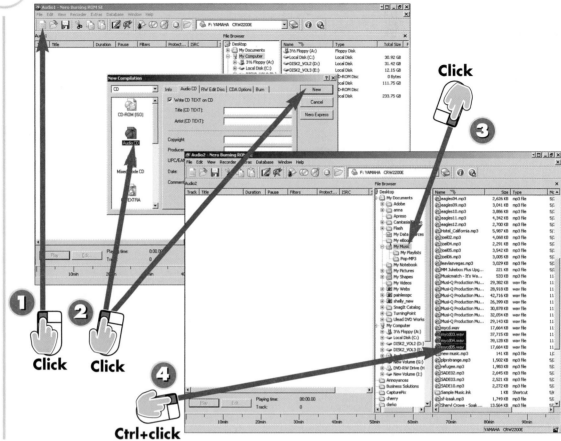

Click

Click

Click

Ctrl+click

1. In Nero Burning ROM, click to start a new CD project.

2. Select **Audio CD** as the project type and click **New**.

3. Click the folder in the File Browser pane that contains the WAV audio files you saved (**My Documents\My Music** or whatever you chose).

4. **Ctrl+click** to select the audio files you want in the compilation.

TIP

Choosing Multiple Files
Select multiple files in the File Browser by **Ctrl+clicking** or a range of files by **Shift+clicking**.

TIP

Scroll through the File Browser to locate your drive or folder and then click the **+** sign to expand it, or double-click it to view its files.

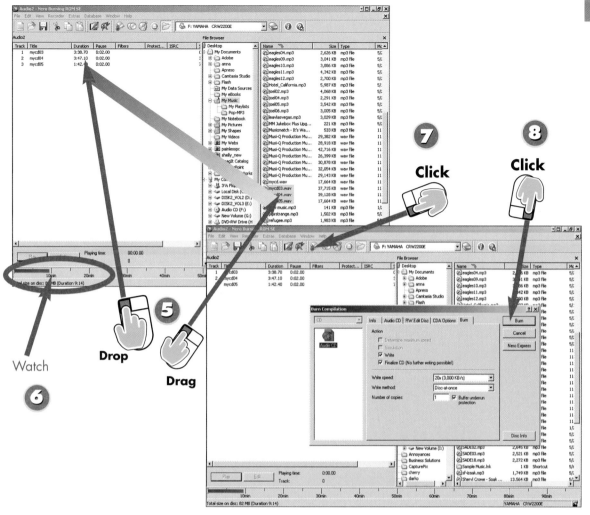

Watch

Drop

Drag

Click

Click

5 Drag and drop the selected files from the File Browser to the Compilation window.

6 Keep track of how much space you have left on the CD.

7 With a blank recordable CD in your destination drive, click **Burn**.

8 Accept (or revise) the options and click **Burn** to record your new audio CD.

End

Extracting (Ripping) MP3 Files

Start

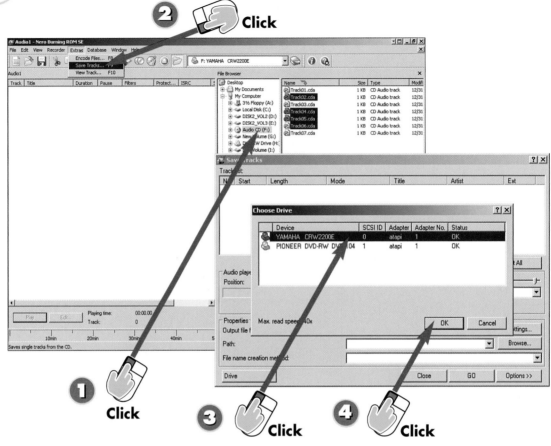

Click ②

Click ①

Click ③

Click ④

① Open **Nero Burning ROM**, insert an audio CD, and click on the drive letter as we did in "Starting an Audio CD with Nero Burning ROM."

② Click **Extras**, **Save Tracks** or press F8.

③ Confirm the recorder that has the audio CD with your music. (The Nero Database window will open again—just click **Cancel** to close it for now.)

④ Click **OK**.

INTRODUCTION

In a preceding task you saved your files in Windows WAV format, which is full blown audio CD quality. Many users want to save their ripped files in the highly popular *compressed* MP3 format, to save disc space and also to move the files to MP3 audio CDs and portable devices. This task shows you how it's done.

Creating MP3 from WAV Files
You can extract or rip songs as MP3 from a disc, or convert (encode) them from previously saved tracks as WAV files. Notice the Encode Files option under the **Nero**, **Extras** menu.

Choosing Different Encoders
There are different encoding standards (compression types) for MP3. Nero uses the most popular ones.

5 By default, all of the audio tracks on your CD are selected. To deselect them all, click elsewhere in the window, then Ctrl+click on one or more tracks to select them.

6 Click the **Output file format** drop-down arrow and choose **MP3** format.

7 Click **Browse** to select a new folder for the audio files (or note the default destination).

8 Select a subfolder (such as **My Documents\My Music\Pop-MP3**) and click **OK**.

See next page

Locating Your Music
Remember that your My Music folder is in My Documents, which is found under your User Name in Documents and Settings (C:\Documents and Settings\[User Name]\My Documents\My Music).

Nero's Encoder Limit
Nero only gives you a 30-day trial version of its MP3 encoder. You can download and buy the full version or use third-party encoders to convert your files. You can download such programs at CNET— **http://snipurl.com/c7sa**.

Creating Music Subfolders
We created a new subfolder in My Music to hold our Pop-MP3 files. You might find it helpful to separate your audio files by file type or genre, and then extract and/or encode them to the appropriate folder to keep them organized.

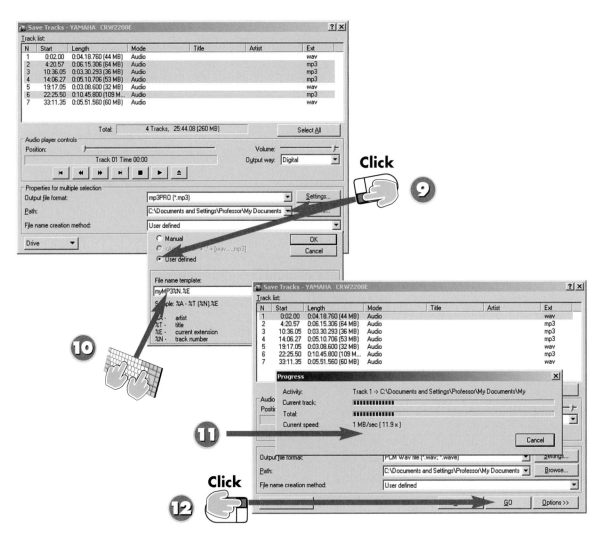

9   Click the drop down arrow for **File creation method** and select **User defined**.

10   Type a name for the tracks like **MyMP3** (or the name of the album or artist) and leave the "%N.%E" extension.

11   Click **GO**.

12   Watch the progress as the files are converted from CD audio to MP3 format.

INTRODUCTION

The process of extracting and naming MP3 tracks is very similar to what we saw with the WAV files. You will find that the resulting compressed files are smaller in size, and so they can be used on portable devices as well as enjoyed on the PC, or burned to audio CD.

TIP

Why You Should Name Your Files
If you don't select the **User defined** option for naming the tracks, they will always be named just Track01, 02, and so on, and you will keep overwriting previously named tracks.

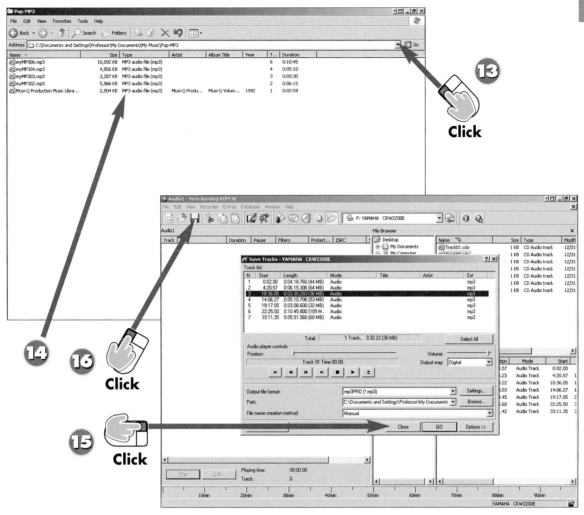

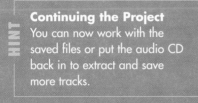

13 In Windows, open the **My Documents\My Music\Pop-MP3** folder, or whatever folder you selected for your MP3 files.

14 Your newly named and saved audio CD tracks are now saved as compressed MP3 files.

15 Click to **Close** the Save Tracks dialog box.

16 Click the **Save Compilation** button and save your project file.

End

Continuing the Project
You can now work with the saved files or put the audio CD back in to extract and save more tracks.

Reopening a Project File
You can double-click the icon for any Nero project file to reopen the compilation in the default application (Nero Burning ROM or Nero Express).

Working with MP3 Files
Once you've saved the files in MP3 format, they can be burned as a regular audio CD (although the quality of sound will still be MP3) or burned as an MP3 disc (as we'll soon see) which plays in many later model audio CD and DVD players.

Converting (Encoding) MP3 Files

Start

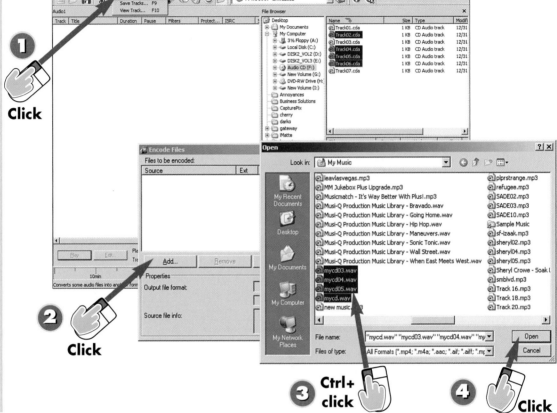

Click

Click

3 Ctrl+ click

4 Click

1 Click **Extras**, **Encode Files** or press F9.

2 Click **Add**.

3 Locate the folder with your saved WAV files and **Ctrl+click** to select one or more of them.

4 Click **Open**.

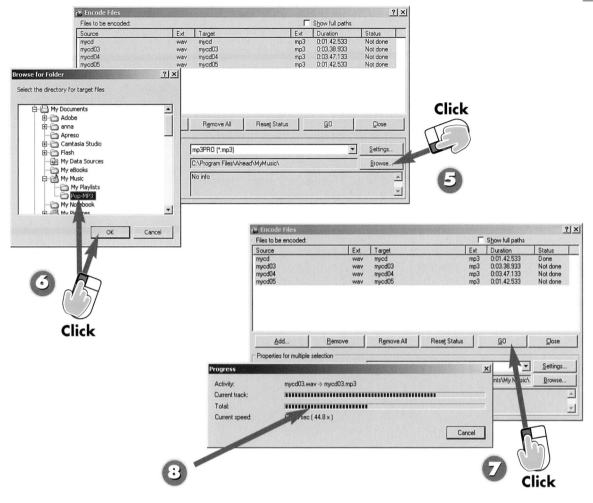

Click

Click

Click

5 With the audio tracks added to the Encode Files window, click **Browse** if you want to change the folder destination.

6 Select a new folder (like Pop-MP3 if you've created it) and click **OK**.

7 Click **GO**.

8 Watch the progress as the WAV files are converted to the MP3 format (and saved to the destination folder).

End

Burning an MP3 Disc

Start

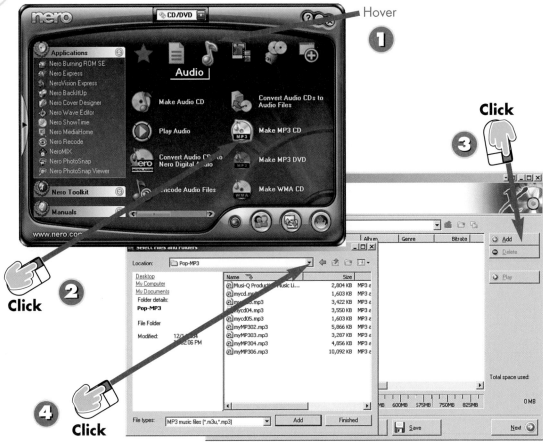

Hover **1**

Click **3**

Click **2**

Click **4**

---

1 In Nero Smart Start hover over the music symbol for **Audio**.

2 Click **Make MP3 CD**.

3 In Nero Express, click **Add** to open the **File Browser**.

4 In the File Browser, click the drop-down arrow in the Location field to find the folder where you've saved your MP3 files.

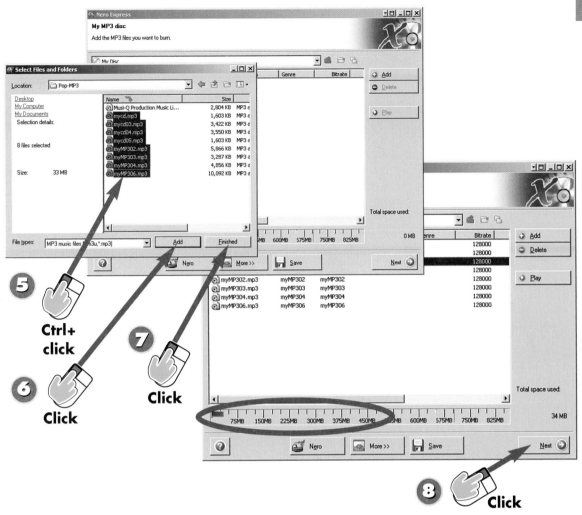

Ctrl+click to select one or more songs to add to the MP3 disc.

Click **Add.**

Continue to other locations where you have MP3 songs to add, and then click
Finished.

Back in Nero Express, check to make sure your disc is not over capacity. When
you're ready to burn put in a blank disk, and click **Next**.

End

Preview Your Tracks
With your tracks selected in
Nero Express, you can play a
track to make sure it's the one
you want, or delete one or
more selected tracks.

**Switching from Nero
Burning ROM**
You can also start an MP3 disc
from Nero Burning ROM by
clicking **Nero Express** after
beginning a new CD project.

Creating a Music Database in Nero

Start

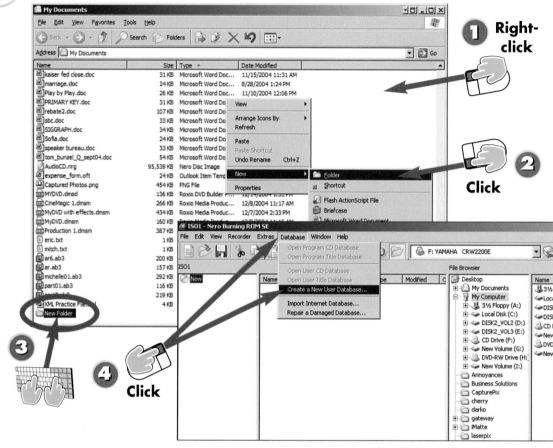

1 Right-click

2 Click

3

4 Click

1. Open your My Documents folder in Windows and right-click in a blank area of the screen.

2. Click **New** and then **Folder**.

3. Type a name for the new folder, such as **Music Database**.

4. In Nero Burning ROM, click **Database** on the main menu and then click **Create a New User Database**.

In all of the tasks in this part so far, we cancelled out of the Database Window in Nero when the window pops up. But some advanced users will love the Database. The Database is like a file cabinet that *keeps track* of your CDs, album titles, artists, and tracks—but it takes a bit of effort to create and maintain, which is why we've dedicated a task just to this topic.

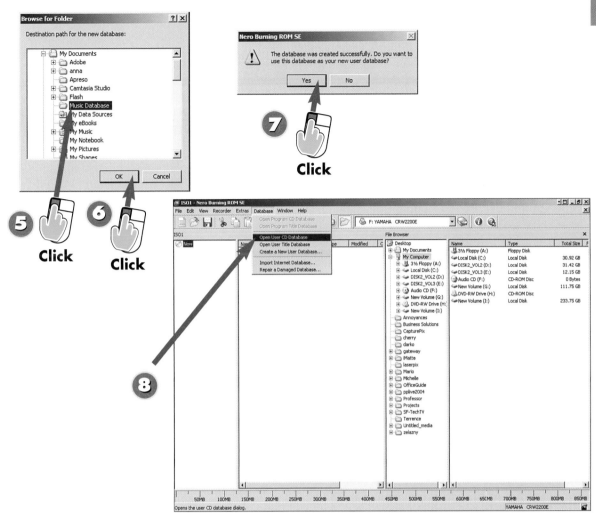

Click

Click   **Click**

Click

---

5 Select the new **My Database** folder you created in My Documents.

6 Click **OK**.

7 Nero will tell you that is creating the file. When it asks you to accept it, click **Yes**.

8 Click **Database**, **Open User CD Database**. Make sure an audio CD is in your drive.

See next page

Why Use the Database?
When you have a live web connection, the database can frequently access online information about an Audio CD and use it to name the songs you extract by album, track, and artist.

Additional Databases
As long as you reference a new folder, you can create as many different user databases as you want. You can also back these up and restore them by having Nero Burning ROM reopen the destination folder as a database.

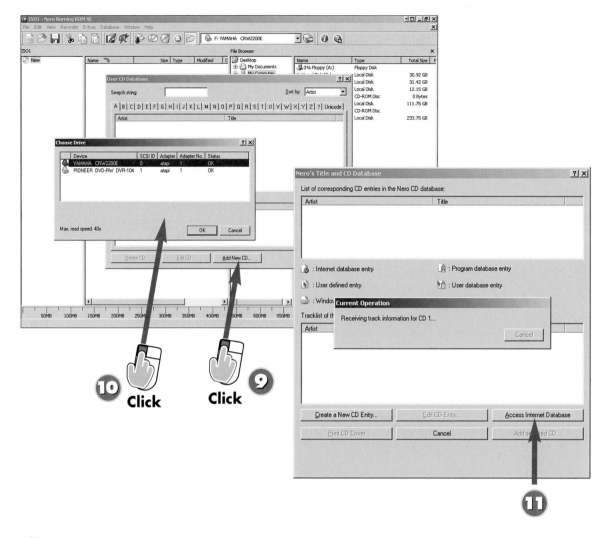

9 Click **Add New CD** and make sure your audio CD is in the drive.

10 If you have more than one CD or DVD recorder, select the one with the audio CD.

11 Click **Access Internet Database**. Nero will go online to locate the CD information.

Turn Off the Database
TIP — If the Database is more trouble to you than it's worth, you can *turn off* the database pop-up window permanently. Click **File**, **Preferences** on the main menu. Then click the **Database** tab, and click to disable the three open Database options.

Accessing the CD
TIP — Sometimes if you forget to insert a disc, Nero will prompt you for it. Select the drive with the audio CD and click **OK** if Nero asks to access the CD.

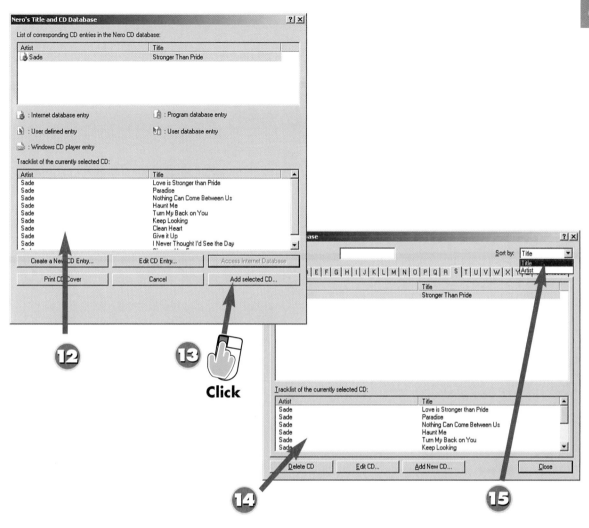

Click

12 Artist and Album title information is found online.

13 Click **Add Selected CD**.

14 Notice that the new entry for the Artist and Album are in the CD Database.

15 Click an option in the **Sort by** drop-down list to sort by Title or Album.

End

Locate Tracks by Title
If you click Database again after closing the User CD database you can also open the User Title database to locate your entries by track title.

Manually Adding CD Information
If you've added information from some CDs and a CD is not found in the online database, you can click **Create a New CD Entry** and add your information manually.

Using the Music Database in Nero

Start

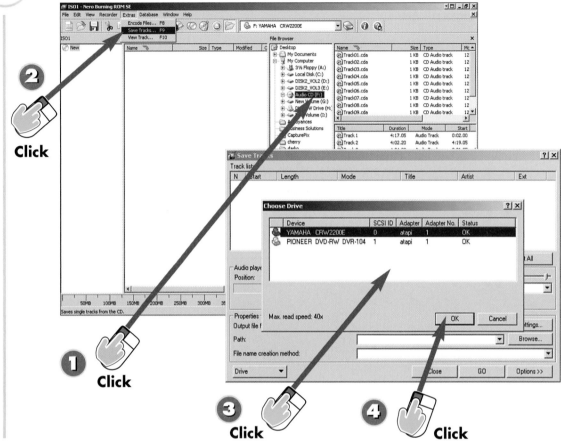

2 Click

1 Click

3 Click

4 Click

1 In Nero Burning ROM, click on the drive letter of the drive containing the audio CD.

2 Click **Extras**, **Save Tracks** or press F8.

3 Click to confirm that the selected recorder is the one containing the audio CD with your music in the database.

4 Click **OK**.

After you've extracted your songs from an audio CD you can see how useful the Music Database really is. (If you haven't already, you should work through the previous task to set up your music database before you work through this task.) With the same audio CD that you added to the database inserted in your CD drive; let's rip the CD to create computer files.

Using Named Entries
You will see the advantage of the database as you extract more music—the saved tracks can be named automatically using the database information.

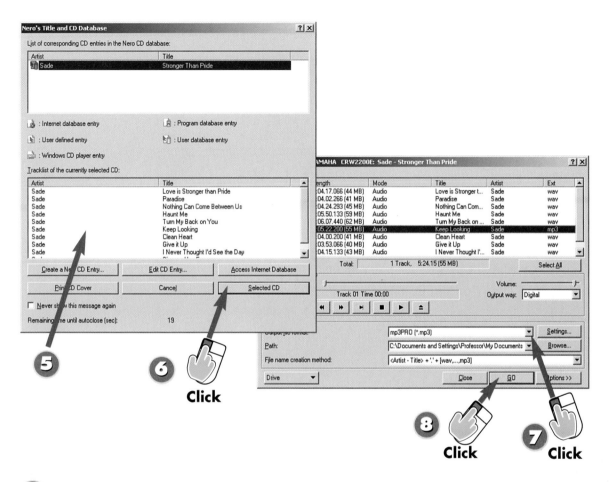

Click

Click

Click

5 Now when the database window pops up, it has your album listed in the window.

6 Click **Selected CD**. Now the songs to be ripped are already named by the entries in the database.

7 Select a file format from the drop-down list.

8 Click **Go**.

See next page

HINT

Choosing a File Format
When you use the database to name your extracted file, you still have the option to choose an appropriate file format. Remember that WAV preserves CD audio at full quality while MP3 and WMA are compressed formats.

HINT

Using Multiple File Formats
You can use the Nero Database to extract and name songs in different formats according to your needs. You could have one folder for full fidelity WAV tracks, and another in which you save your compressed MP3 or WMA files.

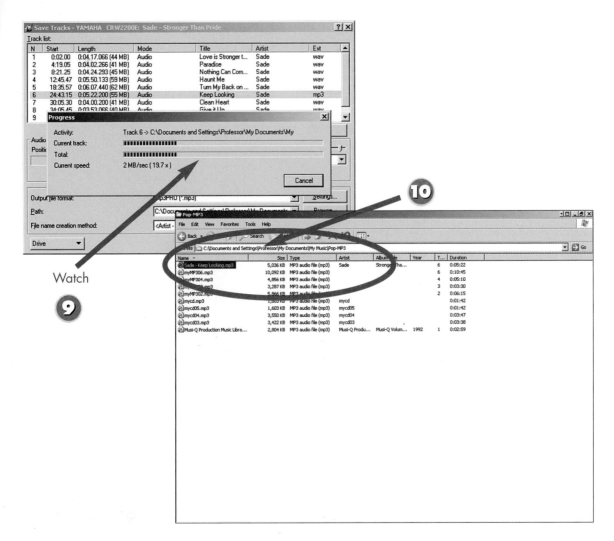

Watch

9

9 Watch as the files you selected are converted from CD audio to the format you selected in step 7.

10 Open the folder where your files were saved. Note that the file has been properly named and even the artist is displayed.

End

INTRODUCTION
As we saw when we began our Music Collection, the converted songs are saved as regular computer files to the destination folders you designate. The difference is that this time they are named automatically using the information in the database.

HINT
Location, Location, Location
If you change the destination folder, make sure to note the new folder so you remember where you saved the files.

HINT
MP3 Tags for Portable Players
If you use the MP3 format to transfer the files to a portable player, the artist, album, and track names will be used as *tags* to identify each song.

Using Copy CD in Nero Express

Start

Click

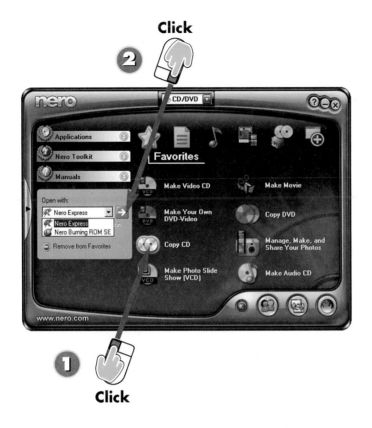

Click

1. In Smart Start's Favorites panel, select **Copy CD**.

2. Click the green arrow to accept the default (Nero Express).

See
next
page

INTRODUCTION

Nero uses both Nero Express and Nero Burning ROM to copy CDs and DVDs. We'll burn a copy in Nero Express and show you how to begin the same process in Nero Burning ROM.

HINT

Choosing a Destination Recorder

In Nero Burning ROM, you need to select a different destination recorder, like an image file, before opening the New Compilation window.

HINT

Using One CD or DVD Burner

If you have only one CD or DVD recorder, choosing the same recorder for source and destination will tell Nero to first copy your files to a temporary directory on the hard drive and then complete the copy.

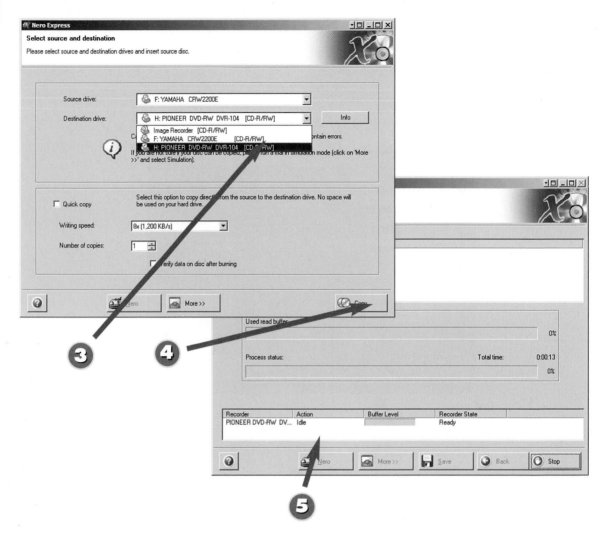

3 Click the drop-down list to select a **Destination Drive**.

4 Click **Copy**.

5 Nero Express begins copying the source disc to the destination you selected (disc, temporary file, or a disc image).

The easiest way to copy a disc is using Nero Express with two CD or DVD burners. But you can also use just one drive, and have the information first copied to a temporary file or disc image.

Copying Options

For a destination recorder you can select a second CD or DVD recorder, or the Image Recorder to create a saved disc image.

Be Careful with Copyrights

Remember that reproducing copyrighted material, whether it is music, video, or computer programs, can get you into a lot of trouble. Check the license rules of software to determine your rights.

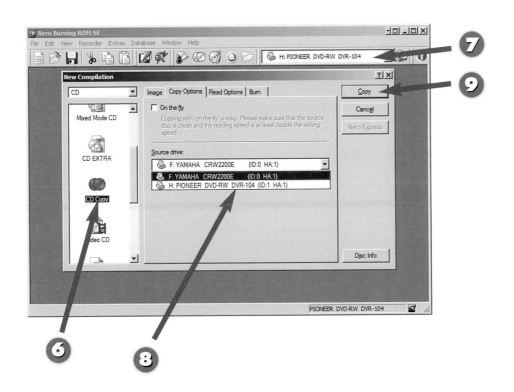

 Or, if you prefer, in **Nero Burning ROM**, you click to choose **CD Copy** for a new compilation.

7 Check the destination drive to make sure it's the recorder you want to use.

8 Choose the source drive from the drop-down list.

9 Click **Copy** to begin the burn.

Quick Copy is Risky
Selecting **Quick Copy** in the panel will bypass making a temporary disc image prior to burning, and may result in errors. If you're really in a hurry, and can afford to waste a blank CD, try Quick Copy to see if your system supports it.

Using the Database in Copy CD
When copying an audio CD, if the Database opens, click **Cancel** (or make additional entries if you like).

Reburning a Disc Image File
By saving your disc image to a file first, you can re-burn the same information again without opening the compilation.

Creating Image Files in Nero Burning ROM

Start

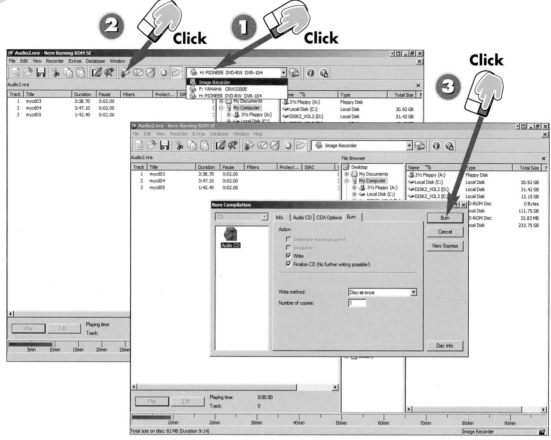

1 With a project open, select **Image Recorder** from the drop-down menu.

2 Click **Burn**. The Burn Compilation window opens.

3 Click **Burn**.

INTRODUCTION

If you like this idea of having image files available to re-burn specific blocks of music or data, here's how to create them from scratch in Nero Burning ROM.

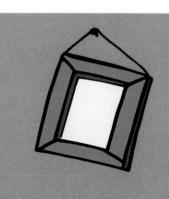

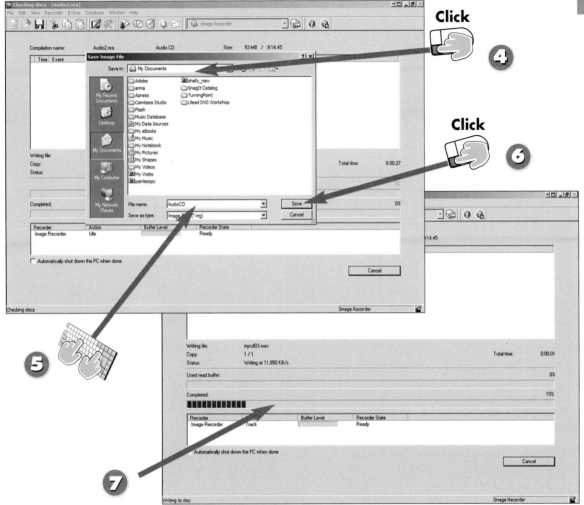

Click 4

Click 6

5

7

4 Choose a folder where you want the image to be saved.

5 Type a name for the file.

6 Click **Save** to create an image file of your compilation on your hard drive.

7 The burning process can be monitored just like recording to disc.

End

Image File Sizes
Remember that image files will be huge—if you are used to filling up a CD (or a DVD!) they will be up to 700 megabytes or 4.7 gigabytes in size. Use smart names—if you use Image1, Image2, and so on you may not remember it.

Nero's Image File Type
The default image format for Nero is *.NRG. An image file can be an audio or data CD or DVD.

Select a CD Burner As the Destination Recorder
When you're ready to burn discs again, use the drop-down menu to change your Recorder option back from Image Recorder to the real thing—or you will only be able to create disc images!

Burning CDs from Image Files

Start

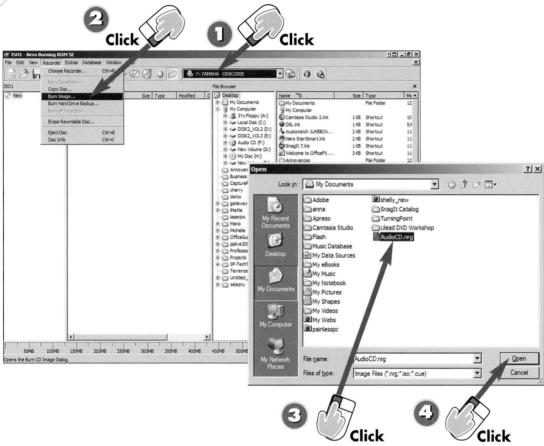

1 Put a blank CD into a drive and select it from the destination panel.

2 Click **Recorder**, **Burn Image**.

3 Locate and click on a disc image file you created earlier.

4 Click **Open**.

Once you've burned or saved a disc image to a computer file, it's easy to re-record the image to disc as many times as you want in Nero Burning ROM.

Be Aware of Image File Sizes

HINT

Before you fall in love with the idea of using disc images frequently, remember that they are large files, and, in the case of DVD images, immense. A CD image file will take up to 650 megabytes (or more for some media) while a DVD image can be up to 4.7 gigabytes in size.

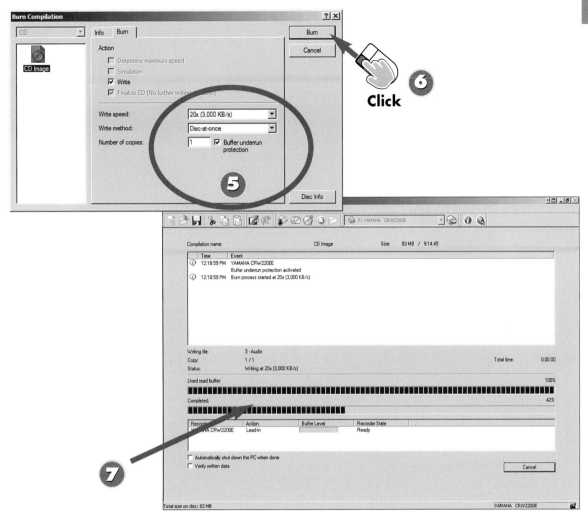

5 In the Burn Compilation window, set your options.

6 Click **Burn**.

7 The disc image file is recorded to the blank disc.

End

Creating a Data DVD

Start

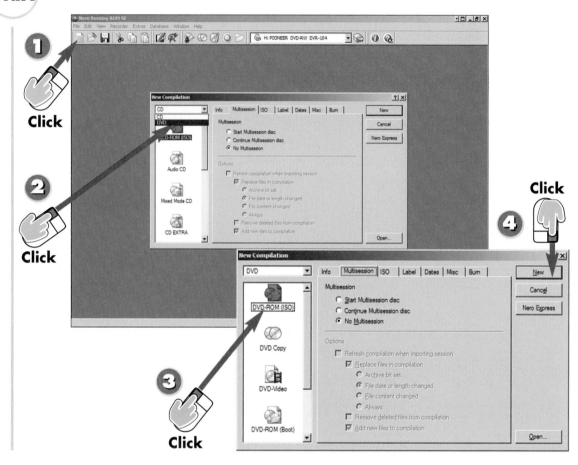

Click

Click

Click

Click

1. In Nero Burning ROM click to begin a new compilation.

2. Click the drop-down menu and select **DVD**.

3. Click the first choice, **DVD-ROM (ISO)**.

4. Click **New**.

INTRODUCTION
One of the wonderful things about Nero (and Easy Media Creator) is the ability to burn huge amounts of data to a DVD recordable discs. This media has gotten very inexpensive and is a great way to back up or safeguard your most valuable computer files.

TIP
Choosing Multiple Files
Nero has a BackItUp utility, but you would need to load Nero again to *restore* those files back to your hard drive. With a data CD or DVD, you can just copy the files directly from the disc to another hard drive.

HINT
Movie vs. Data DVDs
This disc is different from the movie DVD that we will create later in the book. It's like a larger CD-ROM that holds 4.7 gigabytes of data.

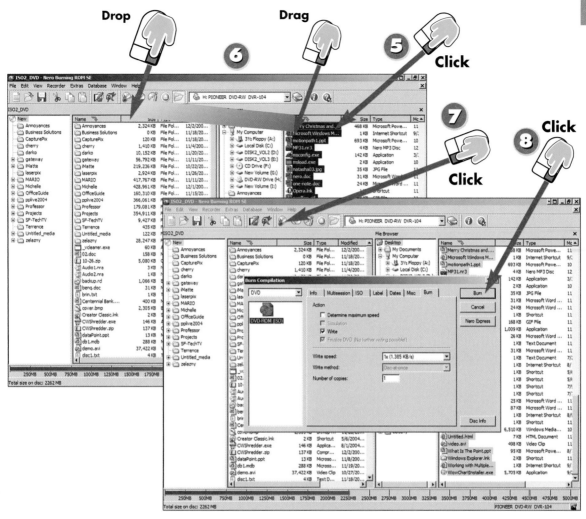

Drop **Drag** **Click** **Click** **Click** **Click**

5. In the File Browser, select all of the files on your Desktop.

6. Drag and drop them into the compilation window.

7. Put a blank DVD recordable disc into your DVD drive and click **Burn**.

8. Click **Burn** again in the Burn Compilation window to begin recording to the DVD disc.

Check Your DVD's Available Space
Check the status bar at the bottom—you probably still have empty space on the disc to add more files since the capacity is 4.7 gigabytes.

DVDs Burn Slower
Notice that the recording speed for a DVD disc is slower than that for a CD. Plan on having lunch or taking a break if you burn DVDs at slow speeds.

Check Your Media
Make sure you use the correct media suggested by the manufacturer of your DVD recorder. Common media are DVD-R, DVD+R, DVD-RW (rewritable), and DVD+RW (rewritable).

How to Create a Disc Label or Cover

Start

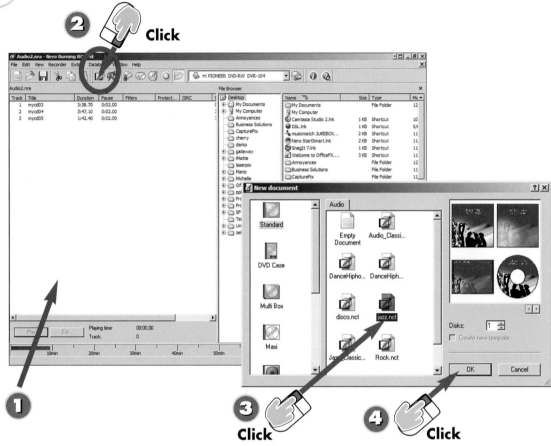

2 Click

Click

1

3 Click

4 Click

1 Open a CD audio or other compilation in Nero Burning ROM.

2 Click to open the **Cover Designer**.

3 Click on a template to preview and select a design.

4 Click **OK**.

HINT

Check the Template Tabs
If you open a data compilation you get multiple tabs in the New Document window—for both Data and Audio templates.

HINT

Cover Designer Uses the Current Compilation
When you open Cover Designer from inside Nero, it works with the files in the cur-rent compilation.

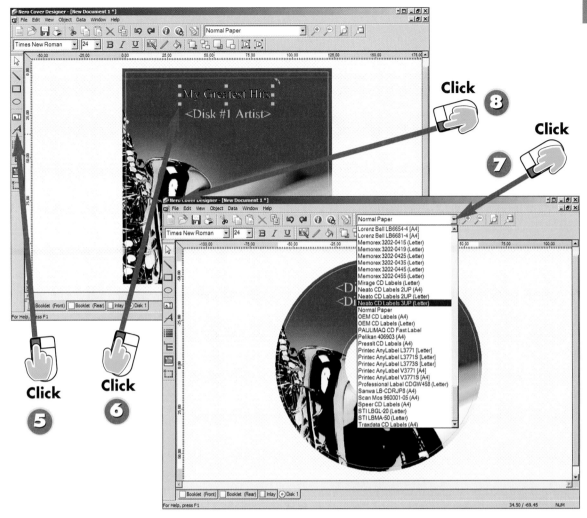

5 Click to activate the **Artistic Text Tool**.

6 Type a title on the label.

7 Click the drop-down menu to access the preset templates for common label makers.

8 Load labels in the printer and click **File**, **Print**.

Remove Unnecessary Fields

Many of the templates come with *field placeholders* to hold disc information. To remove them, select the field placeholder and press Delete on the keyboard.

Preview and Save

If you are using a number of elements (CD label, inserts, and so on), click **Print Preview** under **File** on the main menu to see how it will look. When you like what you've done, use **Save As a File or Template** to use it again.

Label Components

Notice the tabs at the bottom of the window for the Cover Designer let you create graphics for a booklet or an inlay, as well as for the disc itself. Click the appropriate tab and make any changes to the component you want.

Using Media Player to Enjoy CDs and DVDs

In this part, we'll cover the main program in Windows for playing music, Windows Media Player, and introduce the concept of *playlists*. Playlists let you create compilations of favorite songs and determine the order of the tracks.

If you've worked through Parts 1 and 2, by now you've created a music collection (in either Easy Media Creator or Nero, or both). Media Player is a great way to organize the music you've accumulated and enjoy it through your PC speakers—or connected out to your home stereo.

But Windows Media Player can do a lot more than let you enjoy the music you've saved in your personal collection. It can play the videos that we'll use to make our DVDs, and then play the DVDs themselves. It's the Swiss Army Knife of digital media, which is why we cover it here. And, at this point, Media Player is installed on all Windows PCs.

Playlists Organize Your Music Collection

Media Player has preset AutoPlaylists

Set criteria and filters for the AutoPlaylist

Create your own AutoPlaylist

Using Windows Media Player

Start

Click ➊

➋ **Click**

➊ Click the **Start** button and open **Accessories**, **Entertainment**, **Windows Media Player**. If you are connected to the Web, Media Player opens to the Media Guide.

➋ Click the **Media Library** link to open the Media Library.

3 The **All Music** panel lets you select from a number of audio sources, including CD, Internet Radio, or local playlists. Click **All Music**.

4 Select a song, and you can play and pause it with the main controls.

5 To add music files to Media Player manually, click **File**, **Add to Media Library**, **Add Folder**.

See
next
page

Getting Started
The first time you launch Media Player, it will ask you if you want to search for music or other media files. This may take a few minutes if you agree, but it will save the time it takes to import your individual folders. However, it might also put unwanted files into your library.

Searching for Music
You can always conduct a comprehensive search of your computer for music on various drives by clicking **Tools**, **Search for Media Files** (or press **F3**).

Click ⑦

Click & Drag ⑥

Click ⑧

Click ⑨

⑥ Click and drag the scrollbar to locate a specific folder or subfolder.

⑦ Click to select a folder, subfolder, or file.

⑧ Click **OK**.

⑨ Watch as your new files are added to Media Player, and then click **Close**.

Adding a folder to Media Player is actually adding a new set of references to media files in the All Music panel. Once the references are created in Media Player, it will be easy to add Playlists to enjoy the content in the order you want.

What You're Doing

Don't worry about duplicating files at this point; you are just creating *references* to music stored on your computer. But remember, if you or a program you install (like iTunes) moves or reorganizes your music folders, Media Player will need to rescan your system to locate your files and folders.

Click 11

10

Click 13

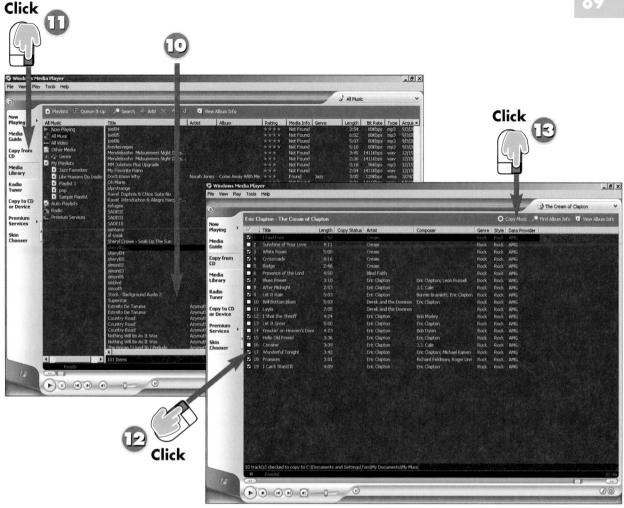

12 **Click**

10 Back in Media Player, you will notice that the contents of your selected folder have been added.

11 Put an audio CD into your CD or DVD drive and click **Copy from CD**.

12 Click to uncheck or remove songs you don't want to play or rip to your local drive (and reference in Media Player).

13 Click **Copy Music** to copy the songs from the CD to a local folder, and be able to play them without the CD in the computer.

End

Setting Options
TIP
If you want to choose the quality of ripped songs in Media Player or change other settings, click **Tools**, **Options**. For quality settings, choose the **Copy Music** tab.

Burning from Media Player
TIP
You can also use Media Player to burn selected songs and playlists, and, with compatible devices, transfer songs and playlists to an MP3 player.

Creating Playlists in Windows Media Player

Start

Click ①

②

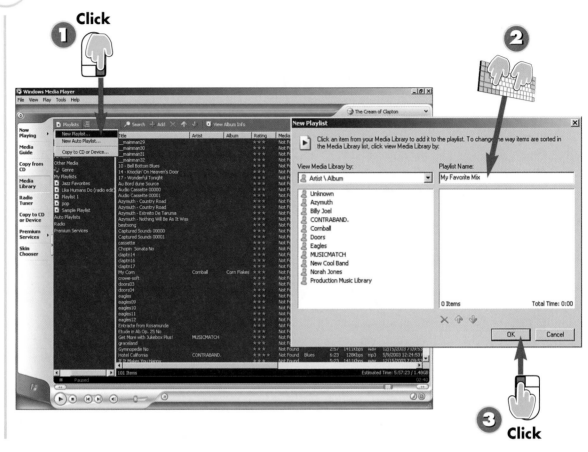

③ **Click**

① Click **New Playlist** in the **Playlist** drop-down menu.

② Enter a name for your playlist, such as **My Favorite Mix**.

③ Click **OK**.

INTRODUCTION

As folders you add to Windows Media Player's library become references to your music files, you can create *playlists* to play your songs in the combination and order you want. This means you can have a different playlist for various occasions without locating songs in multiple folders or moving them around.

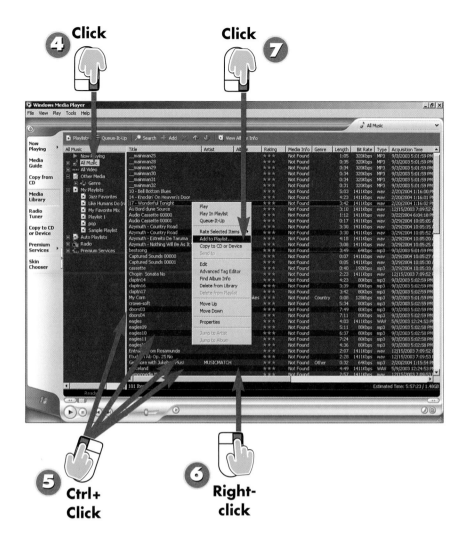

See
next
page

4 Watch as the new playlist is added to the Playlist panel and click **All Music** to
access all your music tracks.

5 **Ctrl+click** to select multiple tracks in the All Music panel.

6 **Right-click** the selected songs.

7 Click **Add to Playlist**.

**Different Playlists for
Different Occasions**
One very nice way to use your
playlists is to rename and assemble them for different occasions.
You could have classical music for
background at dinner, and then a
party mix for Saturday night.

Storing Playlists
A very nice feature of Playlists
is that they're tiny text files that
are easy to store. The key, however, is to make sure that the
music referenced is always in
the location where the playlist
expects to find it.

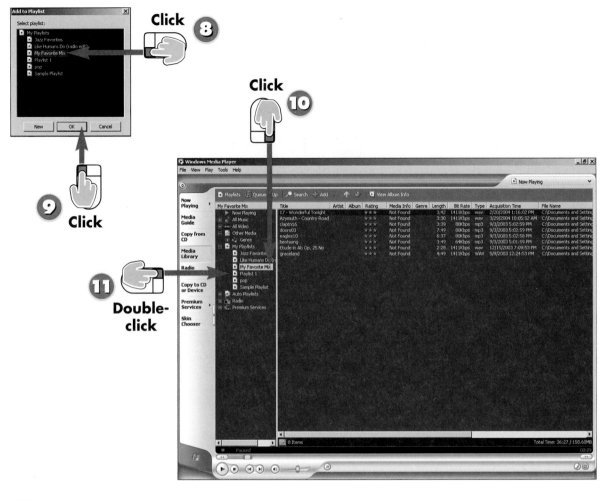

Click 8

Click 10

Click 9

Double-click 11

8 In the **Add to Playlist** box, click your newly created playlist.

9 Click **OK**.

10 Click the name of the playlist in the left panel to open the new playlist in the Playlist panel on the right.

11 Double-click the playlist to begin playing the songs in the order of the playlist. Watch the Play slider proceed as the music plays.

There are two distinct aspects to a playlist. First, there is the ability to play the songs in the order you want, or to locate them by opening a playlist and enjoying each song individually. Then there is also the useful feature of being able to use the songs in one playlist by dragging them into another.

Rating Items
Media Player lets you create ratings for your tracks and then assemble *AutoPlaylists* based on the ratings and other track parameters.

Track Information
To sort or create AutoPlaylists from track information, you'll want to use a tag editor (for MP3 songs only). This lets you attach criteria to songs and sort them by type, mood, genre, and so on.

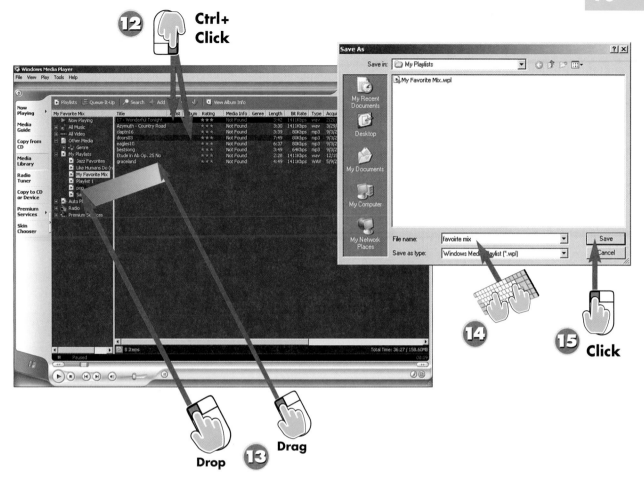

Ctrl+ Click 12

13 **Drag**

Drop

14

15 **Click**

12 Select **one or more tracks** from the currently open playlist.

13 Drag and drop **them** to add them to any other playlist.

14 Click **File**, **Save Playlist As** and type a name for your playlist file.

15 Click **Save**.

End

Track Information

To sort or create AutoPlaylists from track information, you'll want to use a tag editor (for MP3 songs only). This lets you attach criteria to songs and sort them by type, mood, genre, and so on.

Finding Your Playlists

Your playlist is stored after it has been saved in a subfolder of My Music (in My Documents) by default. The subfolder is called, not surprisingly, **My Playlists**.

Playlists on the Network

You are not limited in Media Player, or some other programs, to assembling playlists only from songs on one computer. If you have a local network, you can also add references to Playlists from shared folders you locate through My Network Places.

AutoPlaylists and Tagging in Media Player

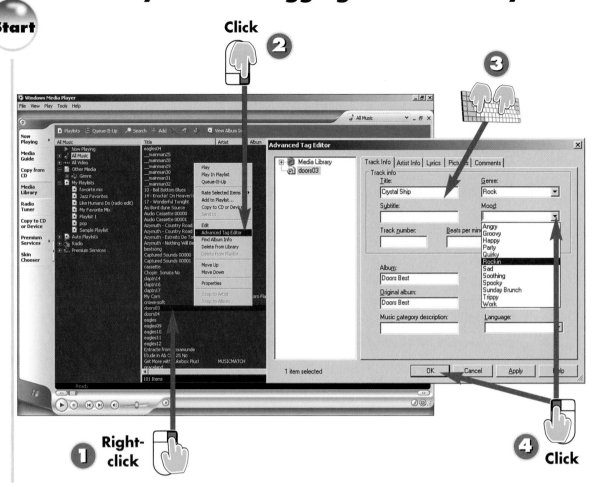

Start

Click ②

③

Right-click ①

Click ④

① In the All Music panel, right-click on an **MP3 track**.

② Click **Advanced Tag Editor**.

③ Type text for the **title** and **album** in the boxes to complete a profile of the track.

④ Assign a mood or genre from the drop-down list and click **OK.**

INTRODUCTION

Like other MP3 players and programs, Media Player is smart, and enables you to track your MP3 music using *tags* (or an index of parameters you set). You can then use or create AutoPlaylists that automatically assemble themselves based on these parameters.

Track Information

HINT

If you acquired the music from a CD or online music store, some of the track information might already be "tagged." You can use the tag feature to revise or add new tag information.

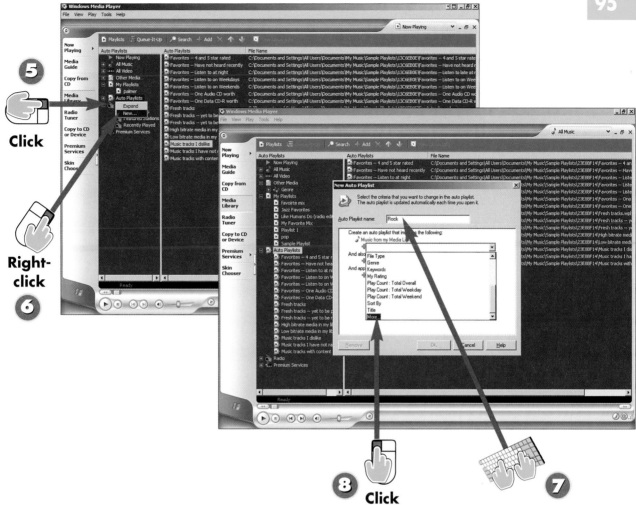

Click

5 Click the **+** sign next to AutoPlaylist to see the preset AutoPlaylists.

6 Right-click **AutoPlaylist** again and select **New**.

7 Type a name such as **Rock** for your new AutoPlaylist.

8 Click the **+** sign to add criteria and select **More**.

See next page

Changing the Criteria
You can right-click any
AutoPlaylist and modify its cri-
teria, or create a new
AutoPlaylist with similar but
slightly different criteria.

Updating Media Player
When you update or upgrade to
a later version of Media Player, it
will frequently have an additional selection of preset
AutoPlaylists that will go through
the All Music collection and catalog your songs by their criteria.

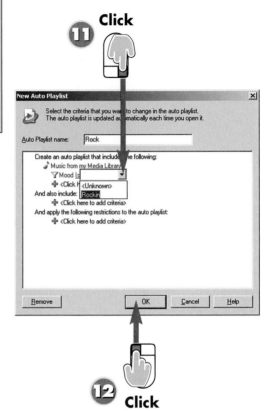

9 Click **Mood** to select it as a filter.

10 Click **OK**.

11 Click the **drop-down arrow** by Mood in the AutoPlaylist dialog box and select the mood you want to set for the track.

12 Click **OK** to compile your new AutoPlaylist.

Besides using the criteria in the preset Media Player AutoPlaylists, you can create your own AutoPlaylists based on your most important criteria and allow them to accummulate references to songs in your All Music collection.

No AutoPlaylists

TIP

If you haven't upgraded to at least Media Player 9, you won't have AutoPlaylists available. They're not in the standard Media Player that comes with Windows XP. See the tip on upgrading Media Player earlier in this section.

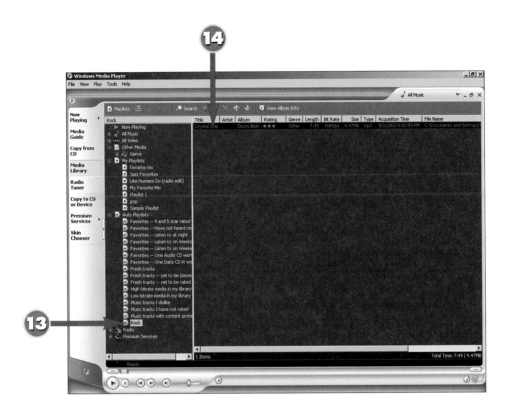

13 Your new AutoPlaylist is among the others in Media Player.

14 The songs that meet its filter criteria are automatically in the playlist.

End

Adding and Monitoring Folders

Click the **Add (+)** button on the Media Player toolbar and review and try some of the other ways to compile and assemble references to files, folders, and playlists. By monitoring a folder you can see if you've referenced all of the latest files that you've added to it using other programs.

Downloading Plug-ins

Media Player also has plug-ins and drivers to work with many different devices such as PDAs, phones, and MP3 players. To transfer your playlists to these devices, get the most current information on Media Player plug-ins by clicking **Tools**, **Plug-ins**, **Download Plug-ins**.

Special Effects in Media Player

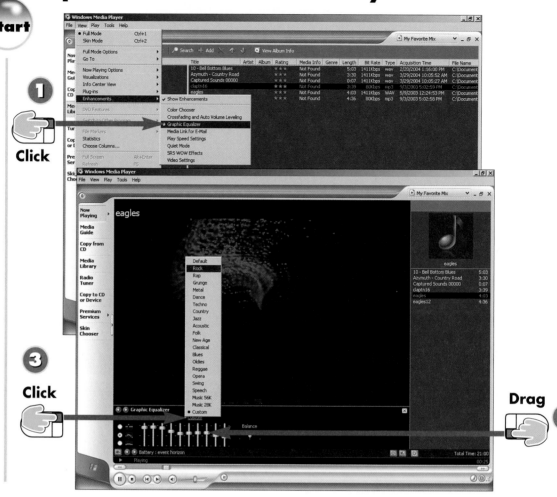

Start

Click

Click

Drag

1. With a track or playlist playing, click **View**, **Enhancements**, **Graphic Equalizer**.

2. Drag the sliders to find the optimal sound for playback.

3. Click the Custom **drop-down** list to select from a number of Equalizer presets.

Now that you've shown Windows Media Player where your music files are located and created playlists, it's time to sit back and enjoy the music. Besides the visualizations, Media Player has a number of enhancements you can use to fine-tune and control playback of your music.

TIP

Equalizer Settings
When you click the drop-down list, you access Equalizer presets. By dragging the sliders to settings you like and then opening the list and clicking Custom, you preserve your own settings. By clicking Default you reset the sliders to the original default settings.

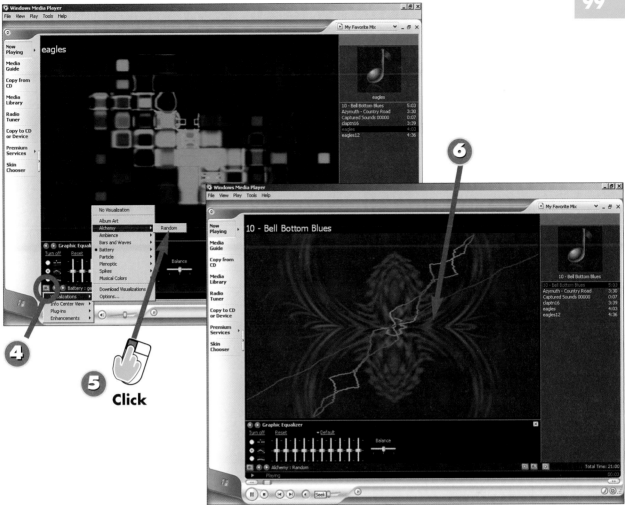

4 Click the button to open the **Now Playing Options** in the lower-left to immediately access other enhancements.

5 Select another visualization category and option.

6 Another visualization replaces the original.

End

Showing Enhancements Full Screen

To expand the visualizations to full screen and hide the Media Player menus, click **Alt+Enter** as the media plays.

Going Big Screen

To show your visualizations on a large-screen TV or monitor, use a graphics card that allows TV output (which many gamers use to play video games on a TV set), or use a large LCD or plasma panel with VGA or DVI input.

Playing Internet Radio with Media Player

Start

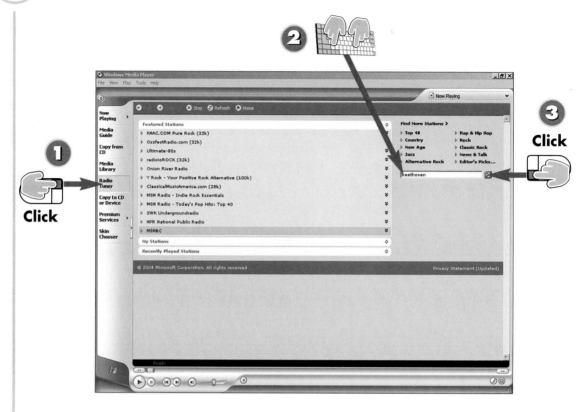

1 Click **Radio Tuner**.

2 Type in a search term, such as **Beethoven**.

3 Click the **arrow** to search.

INTRODUCTION

Among the nicer aspects of having a good sound system in your PC, along with an Internet connection, is finding great radio stations with your favorite music. Media Player makes this a snap.

Capturing Internet Radio
TIP
Technically you're not supposed to be able to record or capture live Internet streaming music, but you can record it to an external analog device, like a tape recorder or even a VCR. There are also downloadable utilities that claim to enable you to capture the music as a computer file.

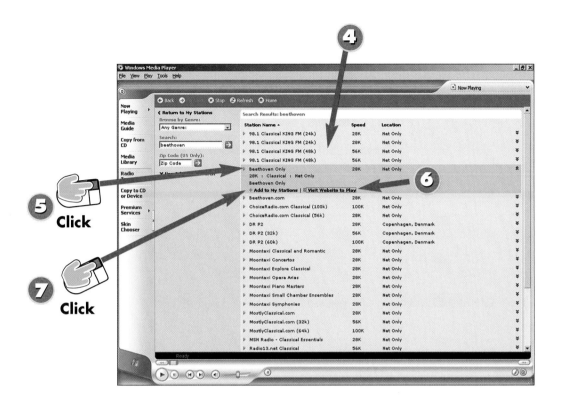

4 Stations playing the searched item appear, along with an indication of their connection speeds.

5 Click a station to get more information about it.

6 Click **Visit Website to Play** to open your browser to go to the station and play the music.

7 Click **Add to My Stations** to create a preset list of station favorites.

End

Check the Bandwidth for Quality

Stations listed in the Radio Tuner show their bandwidth. Although you can listen to some stations with lower bandwidth (even 28K), if you have broadband, you will prefer the quality of the higher bandwidth stations.

Beware of Pop-ups

When the selected radio station opens in the browser, sometimes it is accompanied by advertising, and perhaps even a dialog box asking you to load a plug-in to play the music. If you're concerned about these issues, choose another station or use an antivirus and pop-up–blocking program.

Playing a DVD in Media Player

Start

Click **1**

2

3

4

1 Put your DVD disc into the DVD drive of your PC. Select **Play DVD Video Using Windows Media Player**.

2 After an introductory video, the Main Menu appears. Click a button on the main menu to launch that Title.

3 Click **+** in another Title to see Chapters and click a **Chapter** to jump to that part of the main Title.

4 Click **Play** to play the Chapter within the Title.

End

Since you're going to make your own movie DVD in the next part, let's take a look at how you can play a DVD project in Windows Media Player.

Playback Options

To return to the Main Menu of the DVD, click the top entry in the Titles (and Chapters) list, which represents the name of the DVD. This might be "Unknown" if you burned it yourself.

Going Big Screen

You will also find quick access to the Titles and Chapters on the currently inserted DVD in Left Panel of Media Player, under **Now Playing**.

Making Windows Media Player Your Default

Start

Click ③

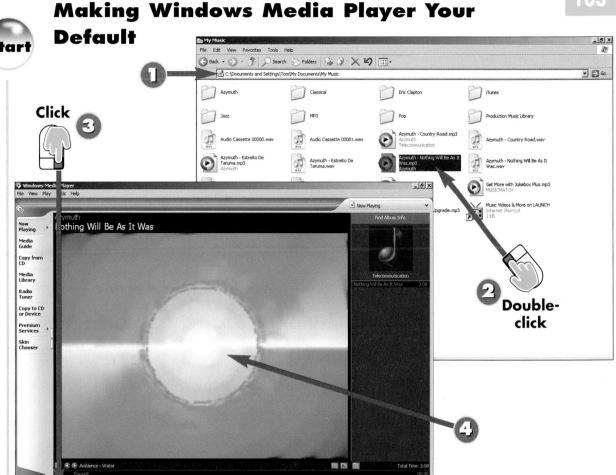

② **Double-click**

④

① In your main music folder (My Music), locate the sound files for the music you've acquired. They'll be mainly MP3, WAV, or WMA audio files.

② Double-click one of the files.

③ Click the **pause** button to stop or click **play** again to continue the song. (Skip to step 5 if Media Player is not the program that opens.)

④ You will see an animated visualization of the music tempo in Windows Media Player.

See next page

INTRODUCTION

In most cases, your default playback program for music and video is Windows Media Player. Sometimes another program "takes over" when you install it, and becomes the default player on your computer. This task shows you how this works, and how you can change it if you want to.

TIP

Resizing Media Player
To see the full menus and toolbars, keep Media Player maximized. If it's reduced in size you might need to move your cursor over the upper-left corner to reveal more menus. You can also minimize Media Player to play music in the background.

You can also enable "mini-mode" by right-clicking on the empty area of the taskbar and selecting **Toolbars**, **Media Player**.

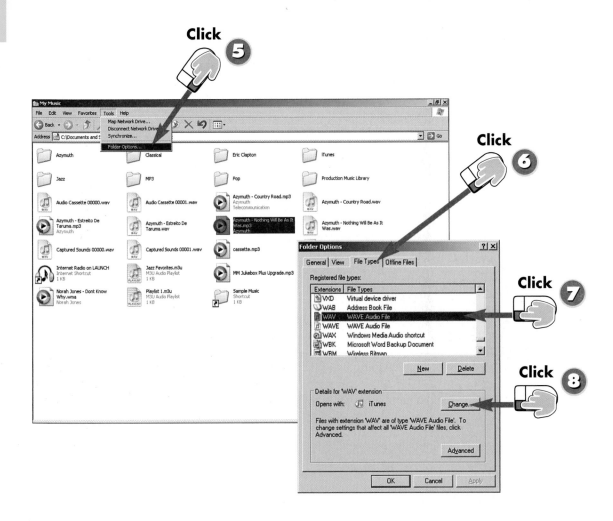

Click 5

Click 6

Click 7

Click 8

5. If something other than Media Player opens in step 3, return to My Documents or My Computer and click **Tools**, **Folder Options**.

6. Click the **File Types** tab.

7. Scroll down to select the file type for which you want to change the default player or application.

8. Click **Change**.

Different Players/ Different File Types

In this example, you can see that the default player for WAV audio files is not Windows Media Player, but iTunes. We're going to change it to Windows Media Player.

Change the Default Player

Another way to change the default player for a file type is to re-install the program and choose the options to make it the default player for one or more specific file types. You can reinstall Windows Media Player or update it by downloading it from Microsoft's website.

Upgrading Media Player

To get some newer features (like AutoPlaylists) you can update Media Player to later versions. Media Player will also frequently prompt you that a new version is available, and you can update it automatically.

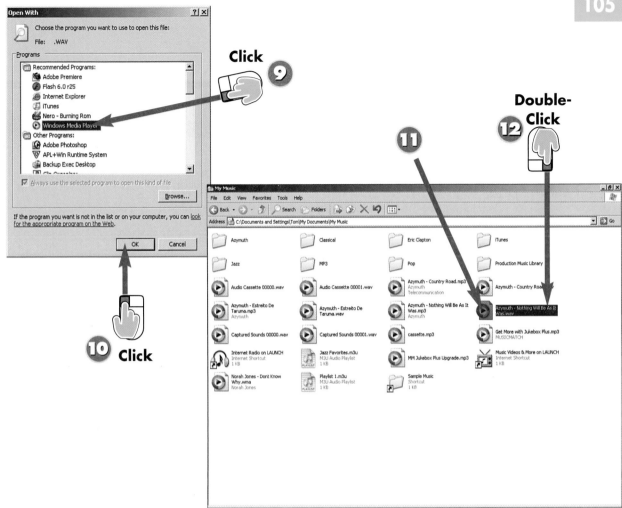

Click 9

Double-Click 12

11

10 **Click**

---

9   Click to select the new default program for the file type.

10   Click **OK**.

11   Reopen the folder with your music to the same set of audio files. Notice that the icon has changed to one representing the newly selected default program or player.

12   Double-click one of the changed files and the new default player will open for you and play the selected song.

End

INTRODUCTION

It's very helpful to have the right program associated with your media files, so that you can locate them in their folders and open the program you want just by double-clicking one of the files. Using the Windows Folder Options settings is a good way to reset these associations if they've been changed by another program.

Weird Program Icons

HINT

If you open a folder and notice that the icons representing the songs or video files have changed, another program has taken over the association. Use the steps here to reassociate the file type.

Other File Types

HINT

This same procedure can be used for any file type on your system, like pictures. For example, if you want Windows Fax Viewer instead of Photoshop to open JPG image files, use the same steps we show here.

Capturing Video and Images with Easy Media Creator

Now that we've burned CDs and data DVDs, we're going to create a true *movie DVD* using the tools in Easy Media Creator. A major part of this is getting video for the DVD into your PC.

There are essentially four steps involved in this process:

1. Acquiring your video.
2. Editing the video.
3. Organizing the material into a user interface or menu.
4. Burning the DVD, SVCD, or VCD to recordable media.

This first step requires that you have a *video capture device* of some kind on your computer for bringing video *into* the PC. The easiest and most popular way of doing this is with a DV (or FireWire) port, which many newer PCs and laptops already have. Most graphics adapters also call themselves video cards, but only a few have *video capture* capability. Beside capture-enabled video cards, there are FireWire (DV) cards and ports (sometimes known as *IEEE 1394* or just plain *1394*), and some USB video capture adapters.

Easy Media Creator will also let you acquire images (and audio and other "assets") for your DVD project and keep them all in a collection.

Whatever video capture device you have will show up in the Capture window, along with other peripherals on your system for similar tasks, such as a scanner or digital camera (for images), and a sound card (for audio input).

Use the Capture Window

Use the preview window to
see your video

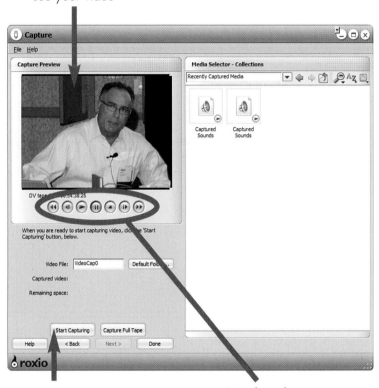

Use Start and Stop Capturing
to grab what you want

Use these buttons to
control a DV source

Preparing to Capture Video

Start

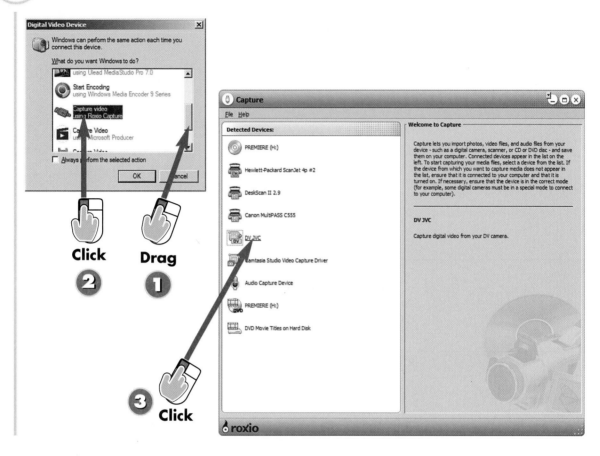

Click
2

Drag
1

Click
3

1 Drag the scrollbar until you see **Capture video using Roxio Capture**.

2 Select to open Roxio Capture and click **OK**.

3 Roxio Capture shows all of the devices in your system capable of acquiring digital media. Click the icon for the **DV [*camcorder*]** (where *camcorder* is your camera's model name) to open Video Capture.

The easiest way to begin capture is to simply connect your DV camcorder's FireWire port using a FireWire cable to the FireWire port of your computer or laptop. When you turn on the camcorder, you will hear a connection sound in Windows, and the Digital Video Device window will open.

Do You Need the Whole Tape?
SmartScan capture and to *Capture Full Tape*, which will grab *all the video on a DV tape automatically*. The segments will be separated in the Collection panel, but this technique will result in huge files.

Setting Up the DV Camcorder
For capture, be sure your DV camcorder is in *VTR mode*, which is like a video tape recorder with Stop and Play buttons.

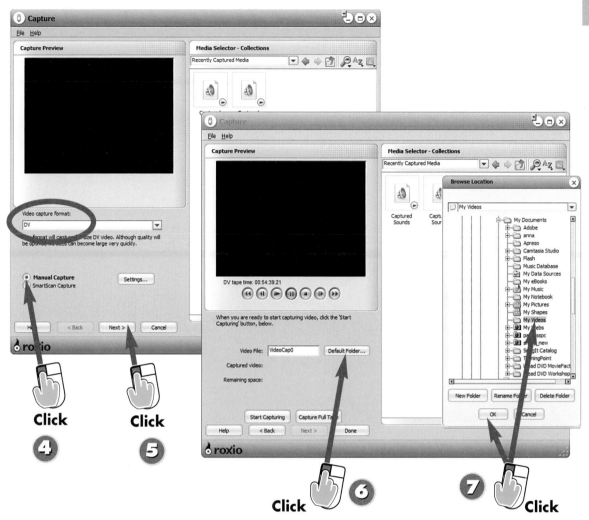

Click **4**

Click **5**

Click **6**

Click **7**

4 Note that the Capture format is **DV**. Click the **Manual Capture** button.

5 Click **Next**.

6 Click **Default Folder** to determine where your captured files will be saved.

7 Choose the **My Videos** folder in My Documents (or another folder), and then click **OK**.

End

Video File Types
AVI is the digital video file type used by Roxio Capture. MPG is the file type eventually used in your DVD project, and what you will *output* in your video editor (in the next chapter).

Naming the Capture File
The default capture file is named for you as **VidCap0**, so that the first file captured will be **VidCap01.AVI**. If you prefer, you can name your captured files manually by entering a new name instead of accepting the **VidCap** default.

Capturing the Best Quality
Capturing in AVI (instead of MPG) format will generally result in cleaner (uncompressed) original clips to be edited (unless you have a fairly expensive capture device).

Starting to Capture

Start

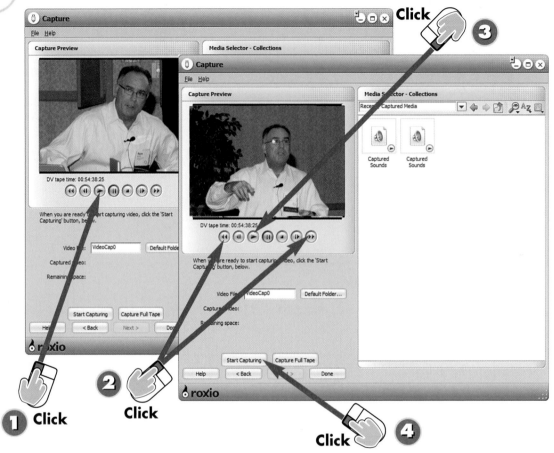

Click ❸

Click ❷

❶ **Click**

Click ❹

❶ Click the **Play** button to preview a DV source. Your footage is shown in the preview window.

❷ Click **Fast Forward** (or **Rewind**) to locate a segment.

❸ Click **Play** a few seconds before the point you wish to capture.

❹ Click **Start Capturing**.

Before capturing your footage, locate and preview it on your computer. Begin capture a few seconds before the segment you want, and end a few seconds after. The preview buttons will work with a DV camcorder. With an analog source you will need to control it manually to see a preview in the window or locate your segment.

Non-DV Video Source

TIP

With an analog (non-DV) video source, such as a USB or graphics card-based capture device, you will plug the **video out** cables from the source VCR to the **video in** port on the capture device. The video cable can be composite (generally a yellow plug) or S-VHS (resembling a PS-2 connector). You will not see a preview in the window until you manually begin to play your video. Push Play **on the VCR** to see a preview. To locate a segment and begin capture, you will need to fast forward or rewind manually as well.

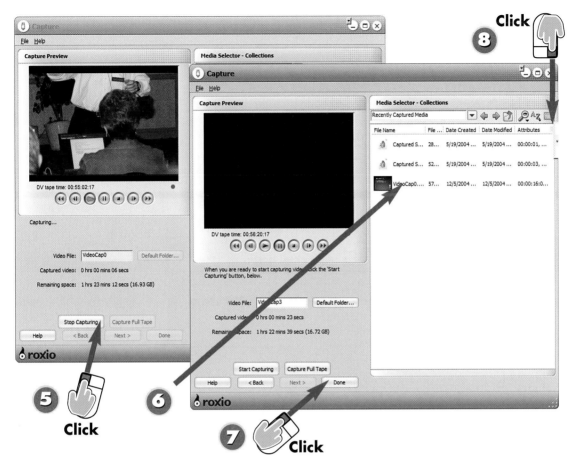

5 Note the spot in the preview window where you want to end capture and click **Stop Capturing**.

6 The newly captured video file appears in the **Recently Captured Media Collection**.

7 Continue with steps 1–5 to capture more video clips. When you're finished capturing video, click **Done.**

8 Click the drop-down arrow on the **View** button and choose **Details** to see file sizes and dates of the video you've captured.

End

Connecting Analog Audio
With an analog (non-DV) video source, you may need to connect its audio output to your sound card, or directly to the capture device.

Capturing from VideoWave

Start

Click

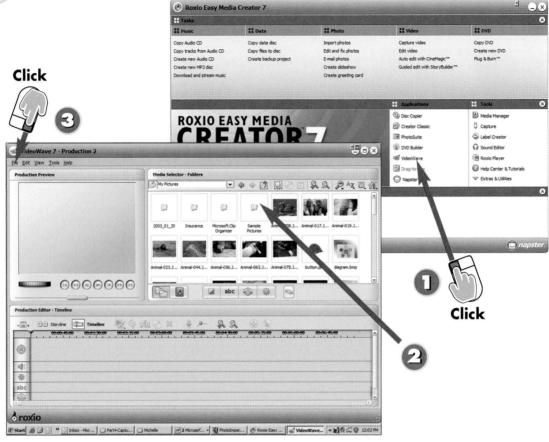

Click

1. Click to open **VideoWave**.

2. **VideoWave** opens to the most recent production (if any).

3. Click **File** on VideoWave's Main Menu.

Remember that the next step after capturing your video will be to edit and organize it. Let's now take a preview peek at VideoWave, the video editor in Easy Media Creator. From VideoWave we can also continue to capture more video if we choose to do so.

HINT

Opening the Capture Window
You can open the Capture window in different ways: by using the menu that comes up when you turn on a DV capture peripheral connected to the computer, by clicking **Capture** under **Tools** in the Easy Media Creator home page, or by starting a capture from within Video Wave.

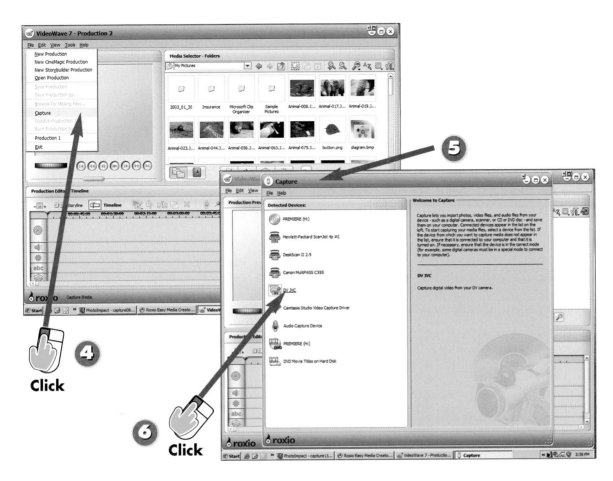

4 Click **Capture**.

5 The Capture window opens over VideoWave.

6 Click your **DV camcorder** to continue DV capture.

End

Capture and Editing
It's important to get comfortable alternating between the Capture window and VideoWave. In the next task we'll see how the Collections panel works.

PART 4

Working with Captured Collections in VideoWave

Start

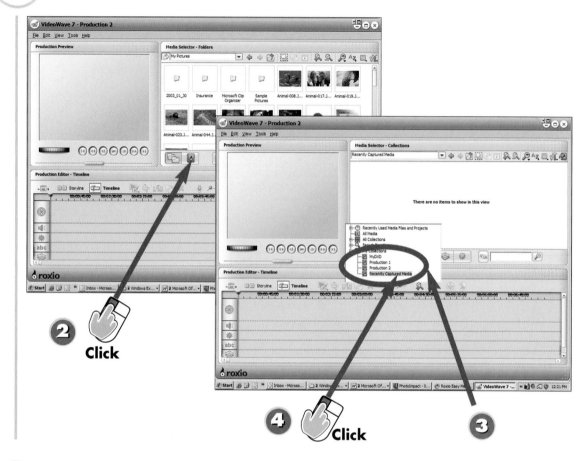

2 Click

4 Click

3

1 In VideoWave, note the default source panel of folders and files.

2 Click **Collections**.

3 The Collections list shows other productions (if any).

4 Click **Recently Captured Media**.

INTRODUCTION

After you've a few video segments in the Capture window, you need to locate them in VideoWave. Remember that the captured video went into a set of Recently Captured Media Collections.

TIP

File Folders and Collections
VideoWave uses the same concept as other parts of Easy Media Creator in differentiating between "real" Windows File Folders (which contain the actual files), and Collections, which you can create and use to simply point to and organize sounds, pictures, and video according to your various projects.

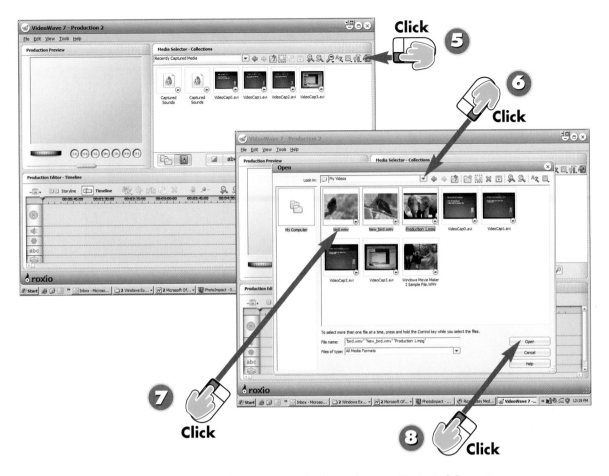

Click 5

Click 6

Click 7

Click 8

⑤ Now your captured video clips are ready for editing. Click **Add to Current Collection**.

⑥ If you have a folder with other video, you can open it.

⑦ Click to select one (or Ctrl+click to select more than one) video clip.

⑧ Click **Open** to add them to the current collection.

End

Collections As Project Organizers
Getting all of your video (or other assets, like images) into a single collection makes working in the VideoWave editor a bit easier.

Collections Are Just References
Deleting an item from a Collection only deletes the reference in the collection to the file, not the video file itself. Use the **Folder view** to actually delete the original files from your PC.

Other Video Sources
We'll be extracting (ripping) video from a DVD later on in this chapter. This task is showing how you would add such video to your collection, or locate other video you may have downloaded or obtained on CD.

Acquiring Still Images

Start

Click ① **Click** ② ③ **Click**

④ **Drag**

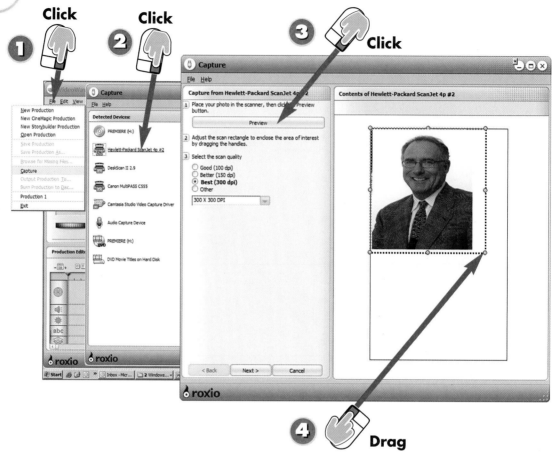

① With VideoWave open, click **File**, **Capture**.

② Click the name of your scanner.

③ Click **Preview** to see how the scan may look.

④ Click and drag the border to the dimensions of the print.

INTRODUCTION

Besides the video you want for your DVD, you may have images that you want to use in the DVD project, either in a slide show or in DVD menus. You can use the Capture window to acquire an image from a scanner or digital camera, and add it to the current collection.

HINT

Using an Image Editor
While Roxio's Capture Window is a great tool that works with VideoWave, you will probably have more success in getting still images the way you want them by scanning them directly into an image editor, like Roxio PhotoSuite (which is also part of Easy Media Creator). See "Cropping an Image in PhotoSuite," **p.200** in Part 8, "Tips and Techniques."

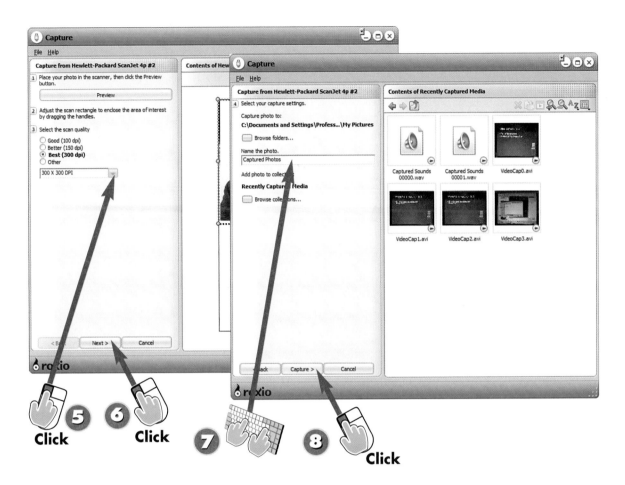

Click Click  Click

5 Set the highest DPI scan quality

6 Click **Next**.

7 Note that the image will go into the **Recently Captured Media** Collection. Keep the default name or enter a new one.

8 Click **Capture**.

See next page

Organizing Your Production
Capturing the image into the same collection as the video will allow you to work with it in the same production later.

Peripherals May Vary
The steps in using your scanner or digital camera may differ slightly, but the result should be the same—you will have images to work with in your VideoWave collection.

Click

9

Click

11 **12**

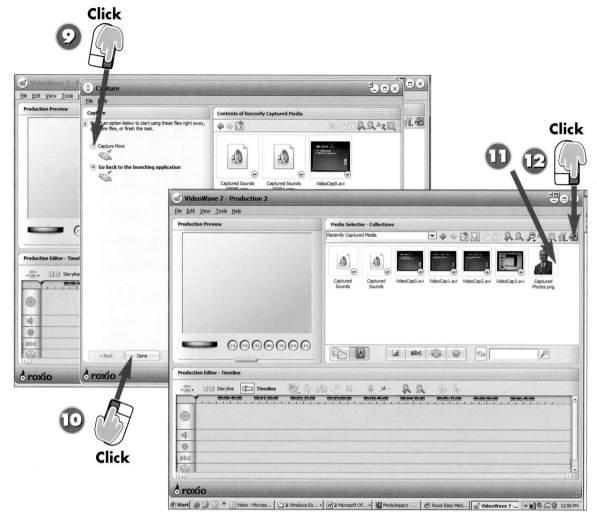

10

Click

Click

9 The captured (scanned) image is in the collection. Click **Capture More** if you have more to scan.

10 To return to VideoWave, click **Done**.

11 The newly acquired image is in our Collection in VideoWave.

12 Click **Add to Current Collection**.

Now that you've captured video and scanned an image, these files will be organized in a Collection to allow you to create Productions. You can continue to acquire video, audio, and still images until you have what you need for your final project.

TIP

Adding to Collections
By clicking the **Add to Current Collection** button, you open the window that lets you accumulate more files for a given collection.

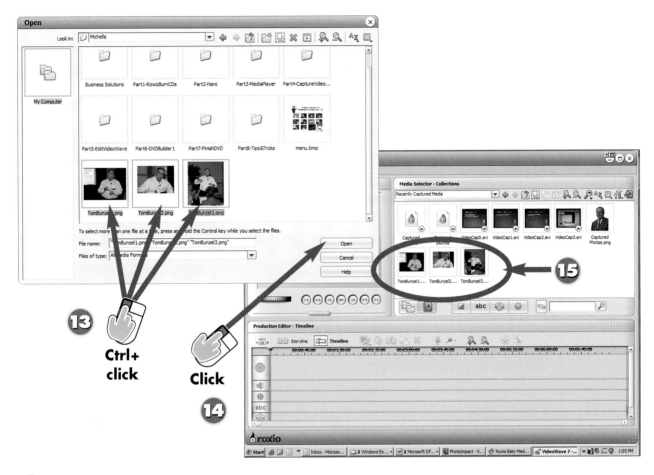

13 Ctrl+click to select other images.

14 Click **Open**.

15 Note that references to the images are added to the Recently Captured Collection.

Capturing Image Formats

The scanned image in this task was saved in PNG format. You can use a variety of image formats in VideoWave including .BMP, .JPG, and .TIF. The type of image file is not as important as the *quality*. For a digital camera this is generally measured in *megapixels*; with a scanner it's a matter of *DPI (dots per inch)* and *resolution*. The higher the quality you acquire, the better the image on DVD.

Extracting or Ripping from a Movie DVD

Start

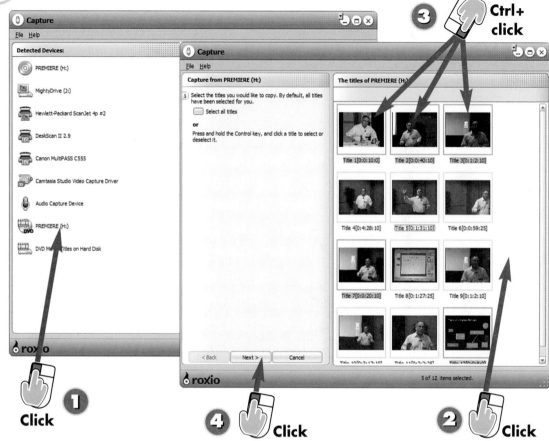

Ctrl+
click

Click

1

4 **Click**

2 **Click**

1 Click the **DVD disc** icon in Capture.

2 Click in a blank area to deselect all the selected files.

3 **Ctrl+click** to select the files you want to extract.

4 Click **Next**.

The Capture utility can also enable you to extract video from a DVD movie disc. You will need a DVD recorder for this task. A DVD-ROM (player) will not support extraction. Make sure the DVD is in your DVD recorder and you have the Capture window open.

Copyright Restrictions
Most commercial movie DVDs are copyright protected and won't allow you to extract video from them.

Extraction Takes Time
There will be a time lag while the files are read from the DVD. You will see the thumbnails for the files appear in the panel one after the other as they are extracted from the DVD.

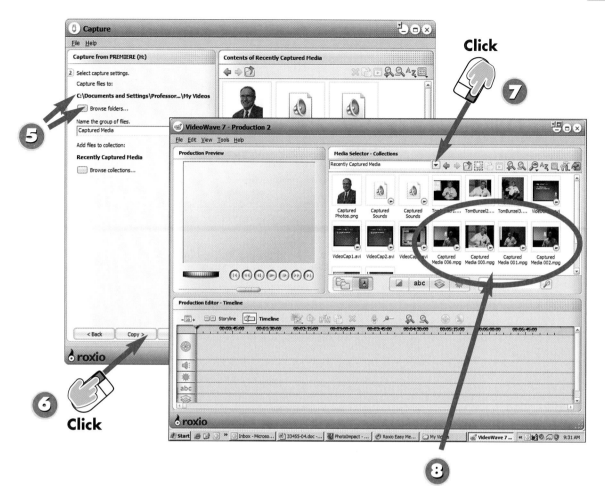

5 Note the folder and collection to which the files will be added.

6 Click **Copy** and watch the extraction process.

7 In VideoWave, open your **Recently Captured Media** Collection.

8 Note that the new files have been added.

End

Saving Your Production

Start

Click

1

Click

2

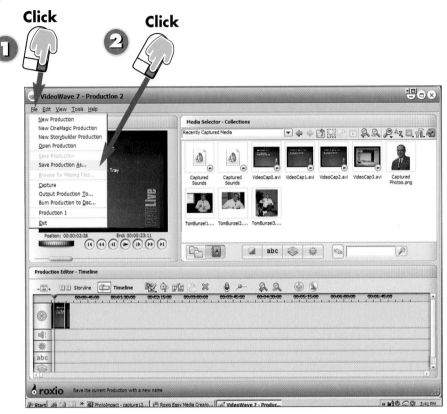

1 Click **File**.

2 Click **Save Production As**.

Once you've assembled the video clips, images, and other files you might need for your DVD, it's a good idea to save your production so that your collection (and future editing choices) are all safe.

Reopening Your Productions
Besides saving the editing choices you made, saving a production lets you instantly reopen it from the **Recent Projects** panel at the bottom of the Easy Media Creator home page.

Click

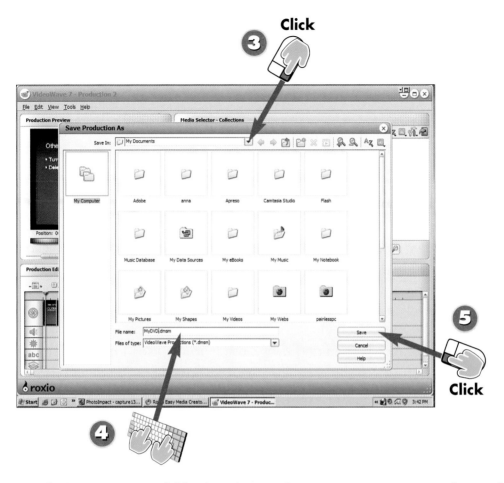

Click

③ Open the My Documents folder (or whatever location you want to save the production to).

④ Name your new production something recognizable like **MyDVD**.

⑤ Click **Save**.

End

Save Regularly

Once you've named a new production, keep on clicking **File**, **Save** regularly to safeguard what you've done. Click **File**, **Save As** to give your production a new name (if you want to use similar collections in another project without overwriting your current production).

TIP

Preparing Your DVD Video in VideoWave

At this point you have accumulated the primary assets for a DVD project: video, still images, and perhaps some sound files to use in the background of menus and slide shows.

Your captured video clips are *raw footage* and there are almost certainly parts of these segments you'll want to take out. The process of editing out parts of a clip is called *trimming*. There are also cool ways to combine your clips, add titles or text, create a slide show, or even extract individual frames to use as images.

For example, suppose footage you capture of your vacation shows your favorite aunt with her mouth open and eyes closed. You would "trim" this footage and leave the part where she is cooking your favorite meal. Then, you might combine that footage with the part where she joined you on an excursion. And you might want to add a title preceding the clip such as "My Italian Aunt."

Everything from the simple task of giving a clip a new start and end point, to combining several clips or images with special effects and titles, is called a *Production*. If you worked through Part 4, specifically "Working with Captured Collections" and "Saving Our Production," you've already added your video clips, both captured and imported, to your Recently Captured Media collection. Now editing and assembling your final video and slide shows will be easy.

When we're done here, we'll move on to assembling our DVD project in Roxio's DVD Builder in Part 6.

Assemble Your Production in VideoWave

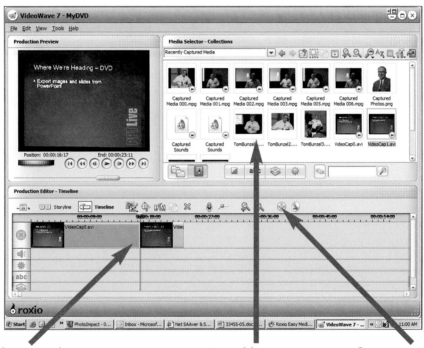

Put together a Production on the Timeline

Assemble source material in Collections

Output your Production as another video file

Starting Your Production

Start

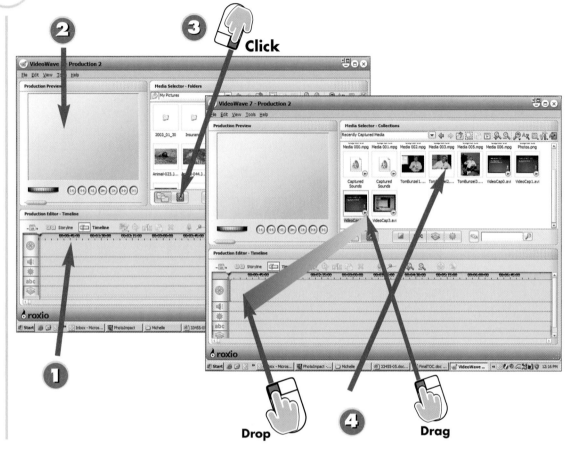

Click

Drop

Drag

1. Note the **Timeline tracks** that you'll use to assemble your production.

2. As your production proceeds, we can preview it in the Production Preview window.

3. Click **Browse Collections**.

4. Your **Recently Captured Media** collection appears. Drag and drop one of your captured videos onto the video track of the **Timeline**.

In the "Working with Captured Collections" task in Part 4, you saw how the collections feature let you organize your production, which was saved for use in VideoWave. Now, let's review the VideoWave interface as we open the project which will become your final DVD production.

TIP

Watch Out for the Folder Menu Drop-down Arrow
Try to refrain from clicking the drop-down arrow for your Folders. If you have a lot of files in your folders, clicking the arrow will put VideoWave into a funk for a minute or two until your subfolders appear.

HINT

Open the Correct Collection
If your Recently Captured Media is not in the Collections panel, select it with the drop-down arrow at the top of the panel.

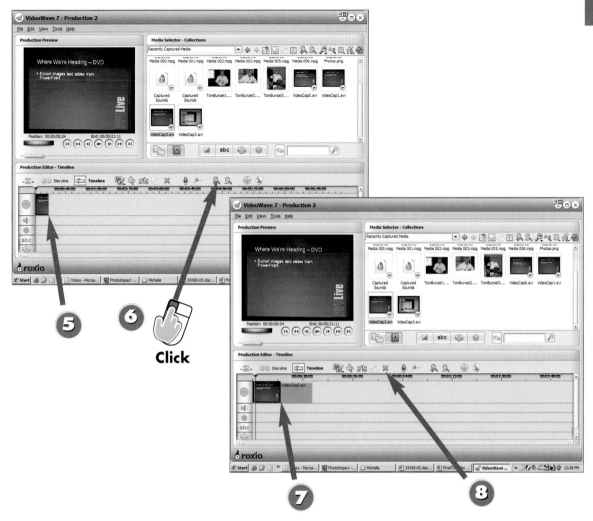

Click

5   The clip goes into the video track of the **Timeline** and is now ready to review in the **Preview window**.

6   Click **Zoom in** two or three times.

7   Your video in the Timeline shows greater detail. This will be helpful if you want to add a sound track or locate specific portions of the video track.

8   Note some of the options above the Timeline tracks. We'll use these to add effects and make changes to selected clips.

End

HINT

Other Ways to Add Items to the Timeline
You can also add clips to the Timeline from the file folders area, but you should get used to working with collections. This will help you assemble clips and images from different file folders for a specific project.

TIP

Details of Your Collection
Use the **Details** drop-down arrow in the Collections window to see your source clips by title, duration, and date.

TIP

Zoom In—Zoom Out
Zoom in to reveal details on shorter productions and to isolate portions for other adjustments. Zoom out in longer, more complex productions to see the big picture.

Trimming a Clip

Start

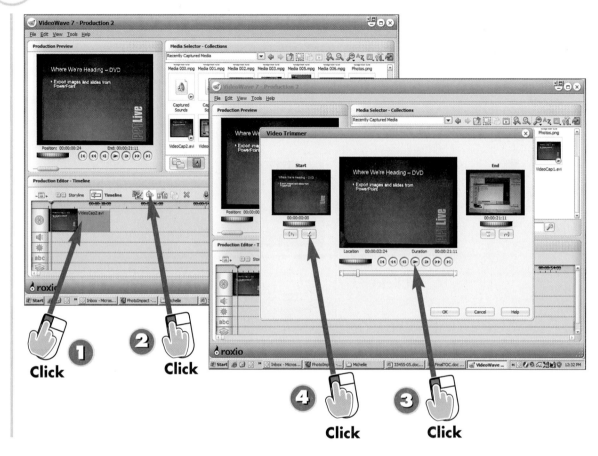

Click 1

Click 2

Click 4

Click 3

① Click to select the clip in the Timeline.

② Click **Adjust duration of the selected item**.

③ In the Video Trimmer window click **Play**.

④ At the point where you want the clip to start, click **Set the start point to current position**.

TIP

Finding a Start Point
You can also locate your start point by dragging over the thumbwheel located in the Video Trimmer or Preview Window and locating the point visually.

HINT

Watch the Time Indicators
Notice that time indicators show the location of the current point in the clip as it moves, and change in its total length.

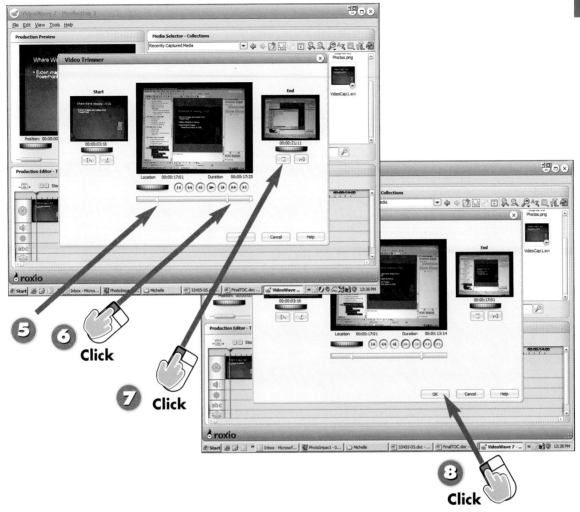

5 Note the new start point on the scrollbar.

6 **Play** or drag the slider to advance the clip to where you want it to end.

7 Click **Set the end point at the current position**.

8 The final trimmed segment is shown on the scrollbar. Click **OK** to return to VideoWave's timeline.

End

TIP

Resetting the Start and End Points
To delete the choices you made and set new Start or End points, click **Reset Start Point** or **Reset End Point** (next to the respective Set Start and End Point buttons).

TIP

Manually Adjust the Start and End Points
You can also manually adjust the Start and End points by dragging over the thumbwheel directly under the Preview window in their respective panels.

Saving a Trimmed Clip

Start

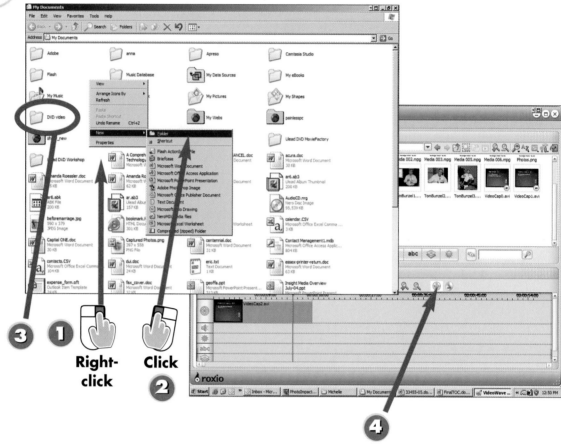

Right-click ❶

Click ❷

❸ ❶ ❷ ❹

❶ Right-click in your **My Documents** folder.

❷ Click to create a **New Folder**.

❸ Name the folder something like **DVD video**.

❹ Click **Output your production in different formats**.

TIP

Preview the Production
Before outputting your production, use the Play button beneath the Preview window to see whether it's what you want to save in a final form.

HINT

Save the Production
When you click to output the production, you are prompted to click Yes to save the Production. This is almost always a good idea (unless you've goofed) so that you can come back and resume the project from its current stage.

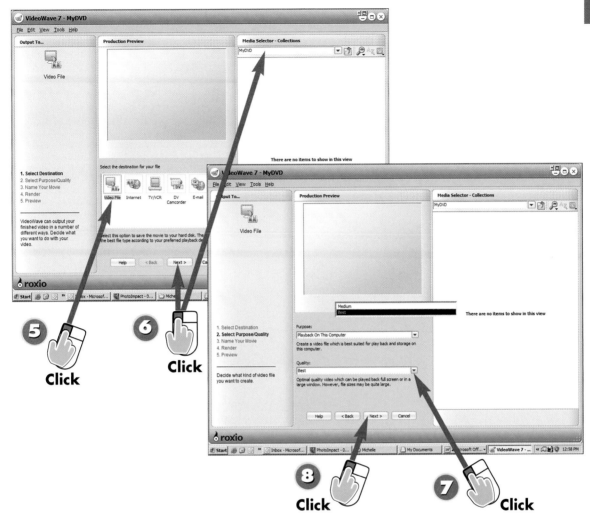

5 Click **Video File**.

6 Check the new Collection named for the project. Click **Next**.

7 Click to select **Best** Quality.

8 Click **Next**.

See next page

Naming Your Productions
If you're going to stay organized, make sure you name your productions something meaningful, not "Production 2 or 3", because, as you can see, resulting Collections are similarly named.

Determining Playback Quality
For now, keep the setting for Playback on My Computer, since you're going to make a DVD with this clip. If you were going to move the clip elsewhere, you would choose other playback settings (for example, for Internet) and change this setting to play back on other computers at different levels of quality.

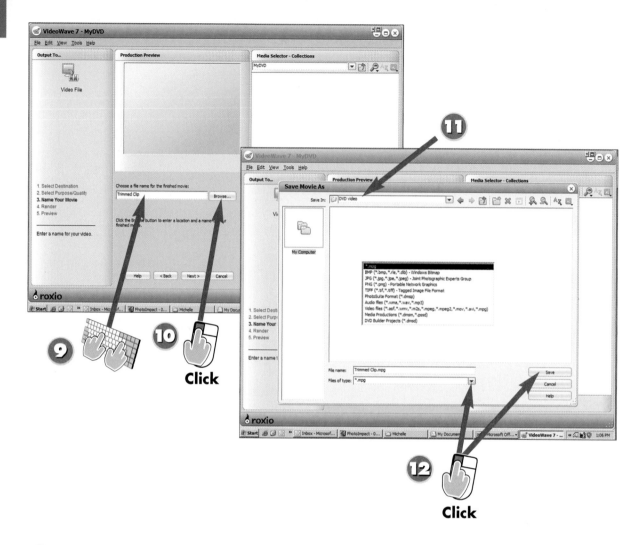

9 Rename your saved file something like **Trimmed Clip**.

10 Click **Browse**.

11 Locate the DVD videos folder you created in My Documents.

12 Accept the default MPG file format (or click the drop-down arrow to change it to another file type). Click **Save**.

INTRODUCTION

At this point in outputting the timeline we're going to rename the final video and decide where it will be saved. We'll use the same folder that we created in My Documents to hold our DVD video.

TIP

Using MPG Files
MPG files will work fine in your DVD project and you can also use them in other PC programs like PowerPoint. You might select another file type (like WMV) if you're going to post the file on a website.

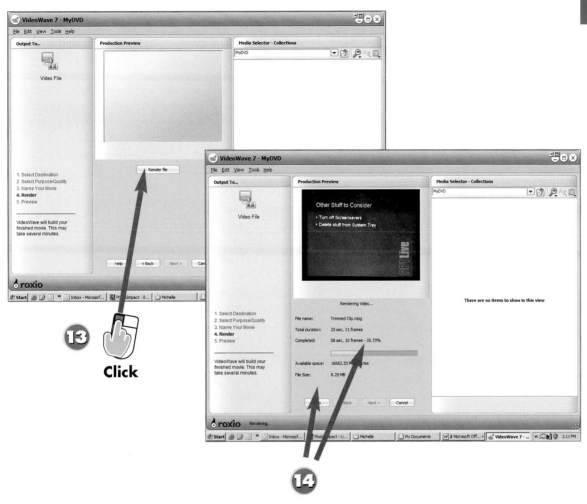

Click

13 Click **Next** once more in the Video output window and click **Render File**.

14 The new file is **rendered** (or saved as a new file). You can watch its final file size change in the status area.

See next page

More Editing Options
You might find it helpful to concentrate on just one clip in your track at a time. By right-clicking a clip, and selecting **Edit**, **Motion Pictures**, you open Motion Picture window which gives you other special effect options. We'll cover some of these in the last task in this section, "Adding Motion to Pictures."

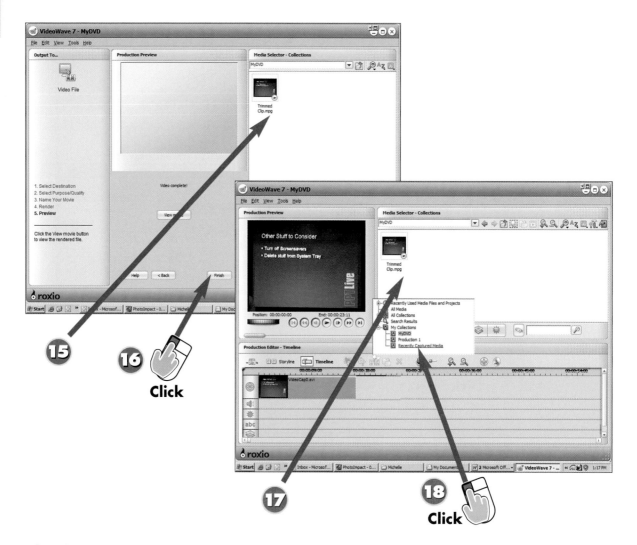

15 A reference to the final movie is added to your collection.

16 Click **Finish**.

17 In VideoWave the clip is available in the MyDVD collection.

18 Click the drop-down arrow to return to **Recently Captured Media**.

INTRODUCTION

When the new movie made up of your combined clips finishes rendering, a reference appears in a newly named collection. Then it's easy to return to the VideoWave main window to continue editing other clips and adding effects and titles.

TIP

Outputting Different Formats

We left the movie format in the Output window set for MPG because we're concentrating on doing a DVD. Changing it to WMV would make it a Windows Media file, which you could compress further and use as an email attachment or in a web page.

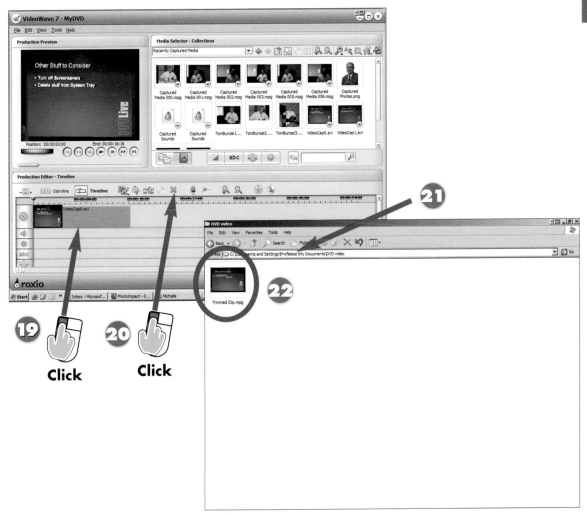

Click   **Click**

19 Click to select the clip in the Timeline.

20 Click **Delete** (the icon with the **X**) to clear it and continue editing another clip.

21 In Windows, open the "DVD video" **Folder** you created in My Documents.

22 You should see your newly saved video file.

End

HINT

The Importance of Outputting Video

Knowing how to save the production as a video file is important as you combine clips and add special effects because you will want to use the final output files in your DVD.

HINT

Back Up Your Video

Now that you know where your captured clips and rendered video are located, you can use the tasks you learned to create a data CD or DVD (in Creator Classic and Nero) to back them up (safeguard them). Remember that saving the *project file* only saves your editing choices—the final video files and source files are very valuable and need to be backed up as well.

PART 5

Combining Two Video Clips

Start

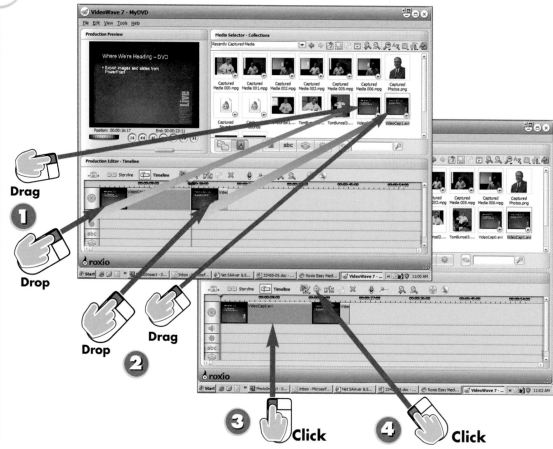

Drag

1

Drop

Drop

Drag

2

3 **Click**

4 **Click**

1 Drag and drop the first clip to be combined into the Timeline.

2 Drag and drop the second clip to be combined into the Timeline.

3 Select the first clip.

4 Click **Adjust the duration of the selected item**.

INTRODUCTION

You may decide that two shorter clips would work well together as one longer video. By putting them together on the Timeline, it's easy to combine them into one complete video. When we continue on to creating our DVD, such a combined clip can play as one complete Title before returning to a menu.

TIP

Using Storyline to Combine Clips
If you don't need to trim the clips, you can combine them easily in Storyline. Just drag two next to each other and click the button to output your production to different formats.

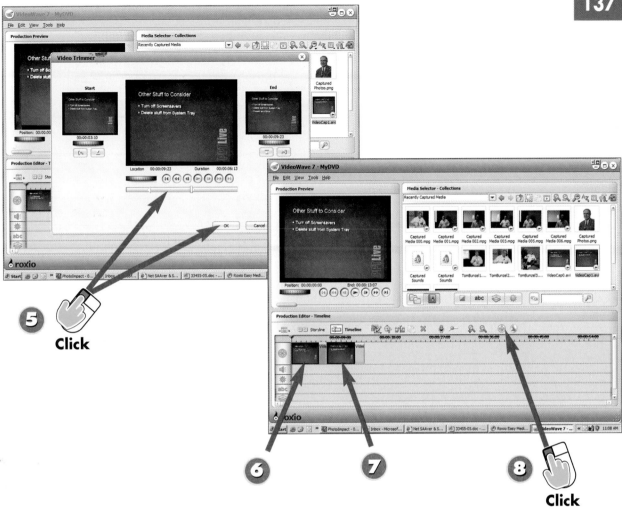

Click

Click

5️⃣ Trim the clip as we've already described previously in the "Trimming a Clip" task. Click **OK** when finished.

6️⃣ Notice that the trimmed clip is adjusted on the Timeline.

7️⃣ Trim the second clip, if you like (following the steps outlined in the "Trimming a Clip" task).

8️⃣ Click **Output production to different formats** if you're satisfied with the results.

End

Splitting a Clip
You can also use the button to **Split media item at current play position**. Preview your selected clip to where you want it split and click the button to the right of Adjust Duration. The clip is split in two and you can select and delete either portion or drag it to another part of the Timeline.

Viewing Split Clips in Storyline
Once you combine or split clips on the Timeline, if you switch to Storyline they'll be in their own distinct story segments.

Adding a Title to a Clip

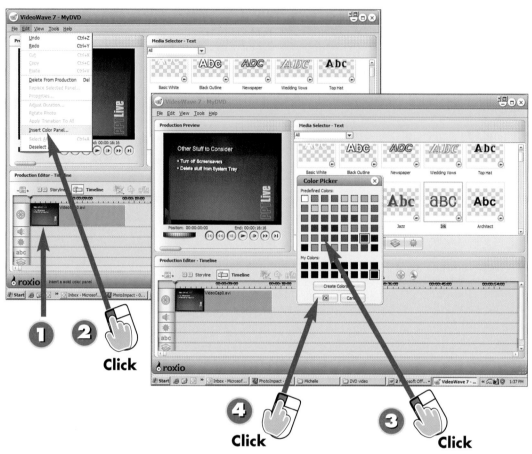

Click

Click

Click

1 Put the clip you want in the Timeline.

2 Click **Edit**, **Insert Color Panel**.

3 Select a color for the color panel background from the **Color Picker** that complements the video clip.

4 Click **OK**.

TIP

Finding More Colors
You can create different background hues in the Color Picker by clicking **Create Colors**.

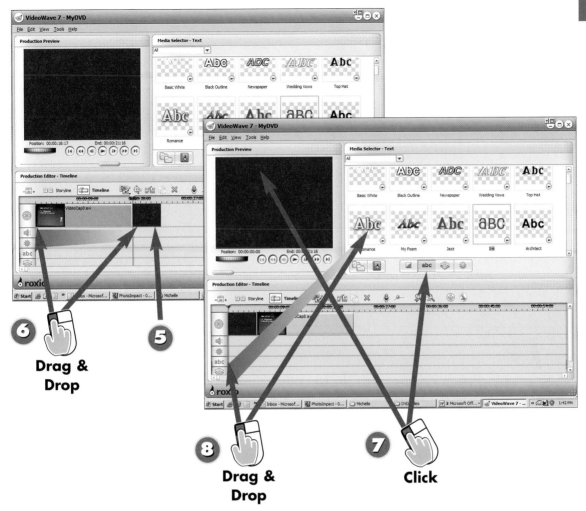

Drag & Drop 6 5

8 **Drag & Drop** 7 **Click**

5 The Color Panel is added after the selected clip.

6 Drag and drop it back at the beginning of the Timeline.

7 Note that the Color Panel is in the Preview window. Click to make sure the **Text** panel is open.

8 Drag and drop a text style onto the **Text** track that contrasts with your background.

See next page

What's in the Preview Window?

TIP

If your color panel or desired object is not in the Preview window, select it in the Timeline (or Storyline). Click **Rewind** below the Preview window to watch the entire production.

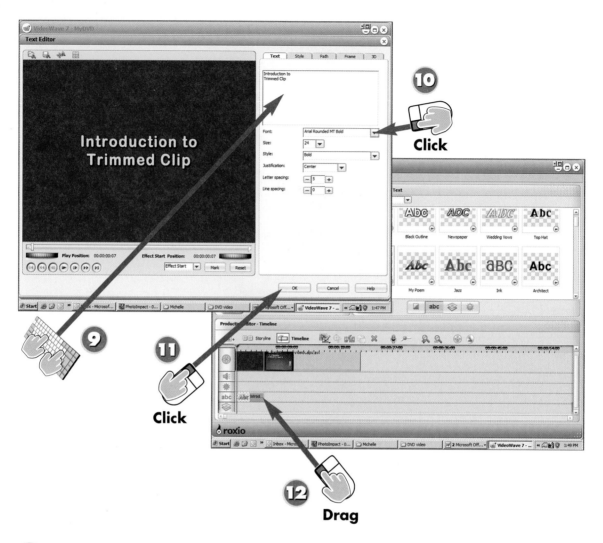

Click

Click

Drag

(9) Type the text you want on the **color panel**.

(10) Select a different font from the **Font** drop-down menu.

(11) Make adjustments to **Center** or **Space** as needed and click **OK**.

(12) Drag the end of the text clip to shorten it so that it corresponds only to the Color Panel.

INTRODUCTION

Once you add text to your color panel, it becomes like another video segment in your production. You can make adjustments to its duration or drag it to another position on the timeline.

TIP

Using Text As Overlay
If you want the text to continue on top of the video clip, don't shorten the clip (drag its right border to the left as seen in step 12) and it will be overlaid on the video segment as well as the color panel.

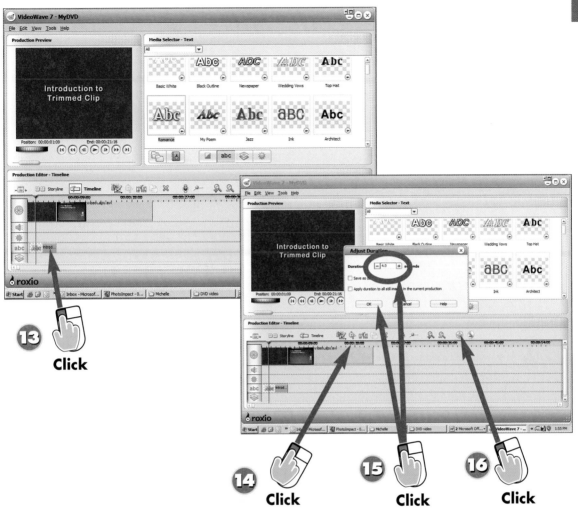

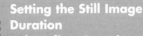

13 Click to select the **Color Panel**.

14 Click **Adjust the duration of the selected item** to open the Adjust Duration window.

15 Increase or decrease the duration with the **+** or **−** buttons and click **OK**.

16 Click **Output production to different formats** if you like what you see. We'll put more effects on the text in the subsequent tasks.

End

Add a Transition with Storyline

Start

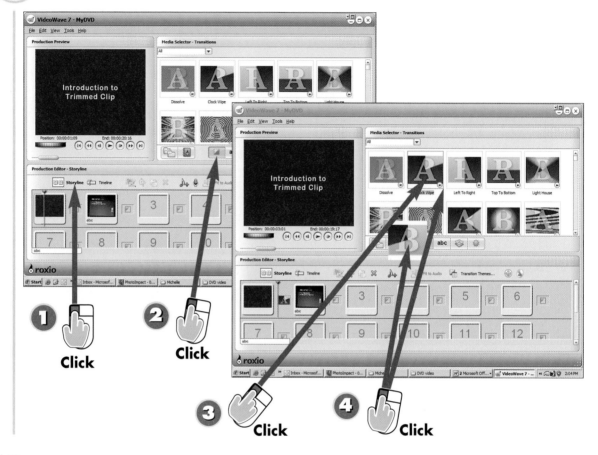

1 Click

2 Click

3 Click

4 Click

1 Click **Storyline**.

2 Click **Transitions**.

3 Select a **transition** in the Transition window.

4 Click its little arrow to preview the transition.

Other nice touches to add to your production are transitions—a series of frames that move a scene from one clip to another, or introduce or exit out of text gradually. Just as we saw with text, transitions have their own selector window, and their own position in the Production Editor.

HINT

Why Use Storyline for Transitions?

You can also add a transition within the Timeline but it's much easier in Storyline. You can see the results by clicking Timeline again when the transition has been added. To add a transition to the Timeline, use the transition track.

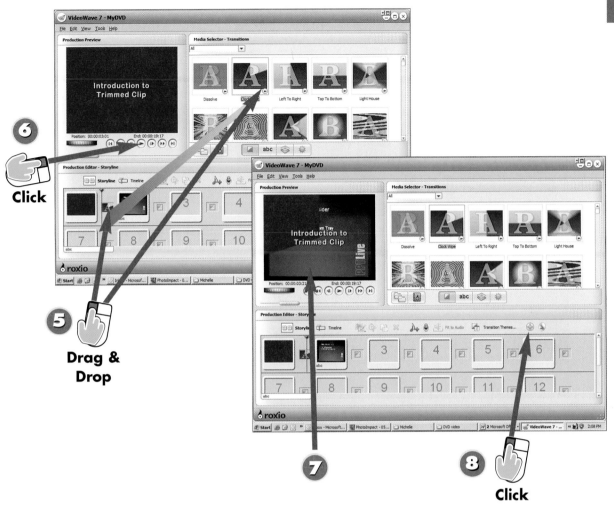

Click

Drag & Drop

Click

5 Drag the selected **transition** and drop it between the clip and the color panel.

6 Click **Play**.

7 Watch the **Preview window** to see the transition.

8 Click **Output production to different formats** if you're satisfied with the results.

End

Using Overlay or Effects

Start

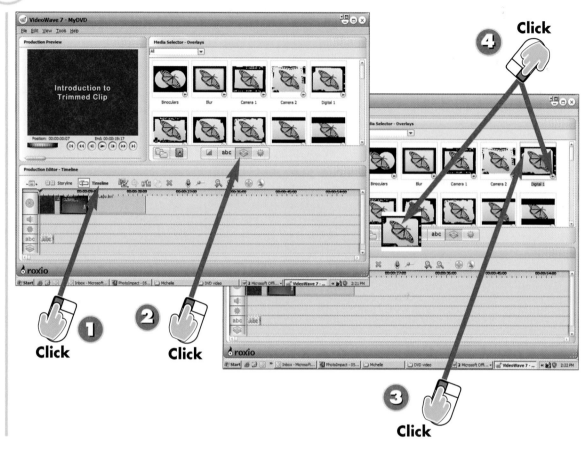

① **Click**

② **Click**

③ **Click**

④ **Click**

① Click **Timeline**.

② Click **Overlays**.

③ Select an **Overlay**.

④ Click its little **arrow** to preview the overlay.

VideoWave also gives you some nice artistic touches that you can experiment with and add to individual clips or entire productions. These are similar to "filters" used by graphics programs and they can apply different textures, cutouts, or designs to one or several selected clips.

TIP

Adding Your Overlays
You can add Overlays in the Timeline or Storyline. To add them in Storyline, just drop them directly on top of the segments you want them to affect.

TIP

Saving Incrementally
Use the **File**, **Save As** option every so often as you are adding effects and transitions to the production. Saving the production at various stages using different names for the saved file keeps different versions of your production available for editing.

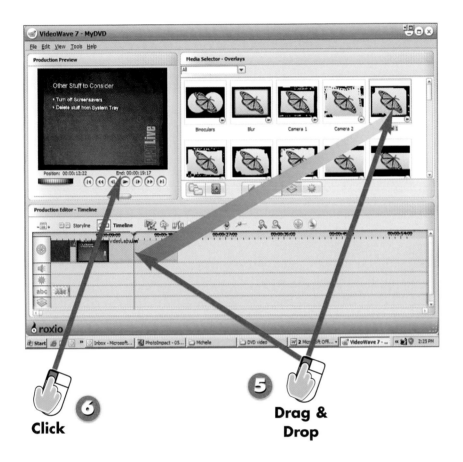

Click ⑥

⑤ **Drag & Drop**

⑤ Drag and drop the **overlay** onto a clip.

⑥ Click **Preview** to see how the overlay will affect the clip.

See next page

Multiple Effects and Rendering Time
The more effects of various types that you add to the project, the longer it will take to render when you output the timeline to a new video file.

Combining Effects and Overlays
Each Storyline segment can have one effect and one overlay. If you try to add a second effect or overlay, you will prompted whether you want to replace the one that has already been applied.

Click

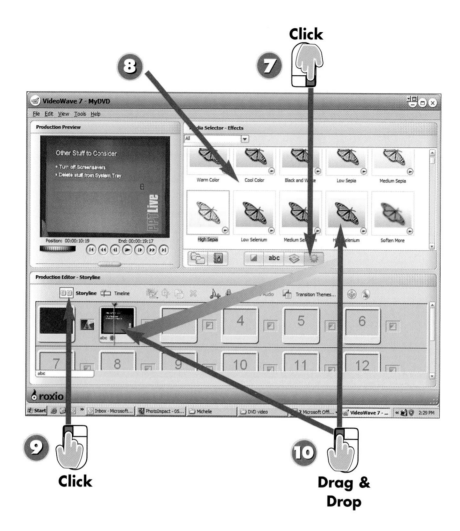

Click

Drag & Drop

7 Click **Effects**.

8 Look through the Effects Panel and choose an effect to apply.

9 Click **Storyline**.

10 Drag and drop an effect on a **Story segment**.

End

Applying Transition Themes

Start

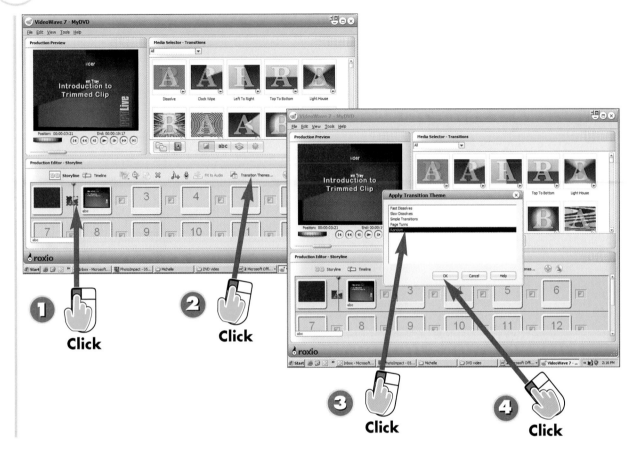

Click   **Click**   **Click**   **Click**

1. Click the **Transition** in the Storyline.

2. Click **Transition Themes**.

3. Select a **Random Transition**.

4. Click **OK**. Click **Yes** to accept the change and/or apply the selected transition to all transitions in the production.

End

INTRODUCTION

You can change one transition to another quickly by using Transition Themes or quickly apply a single different transition or random transitions to the entire production.

TIP

Using Transition Themes
Transition Themes are just a quick way to overwrite the transitions you've already picked when you add a transition using the Storyline. By using a theme, you let VideoWave choose transitions for you by selecting to change all of your transitions to one single transition theme, or to just be *random*.

Saving a Video Frame As an Image

Start

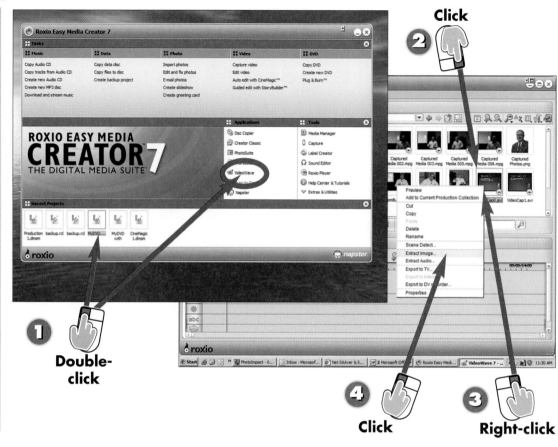

Click

2

1 Double-click

4 Click

3 Right-click

1 On the **Roxio Home Page**, double-click your production. Or, just click to reopen **VideoWave**.

2 Select the clip in Collections from which you want to extract a frame.

3 Right-click the clip **thumbnail**.

4 Click **Extract Image**.

After you've worked with a project for a while you might decide you could use just one frame from one of your clips (or final videos) as a still image. This might come in handy when you create menus for the DVD (in the next part), or to create a slideshow production. Reopen your production in VideoWave to get started.

TIP

Locating the Right Clip
Remember to click **Browse** to find the collection that has the clip you want to extract the image from.

TIP

Extracting Audio
Notice that right-click menu also contains an option that lets you **extract audio**. Follow these same steps to save the sound from a video clip as a separate file.

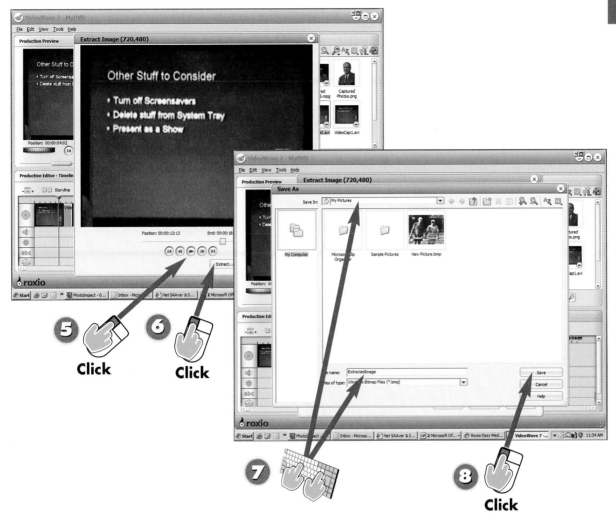

Click   **Click**

Click

5 Click to play the clip in the Extract Image window to locate the frame you want.

6 Click **Extract**.

7 Note the folder location of the saved file. Type a name for the file.

8 Click **Save**.

See next page

Extraction Issues

TIP

You may find that certain videos may have the Extract Image option grayed out or disabled. In this case you can bring video into the Timeline and click to output and save it as another video file (under a new name). Open the new file and you should be able to extract an image.

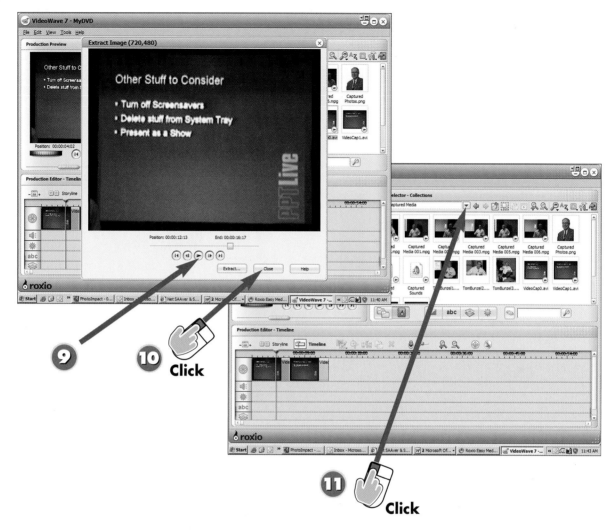

Click

Click

9️⃣ Continue to play and extract images.

🔟 When you're done extracting frames, click **Close**.

1️⃣1️⃣ Click the drop-down arrow for **Collections**.

HINT

Where's the Image?
Your extracted image won't be in the Recently Captured Media collection. It will be in the collection named for the current production.

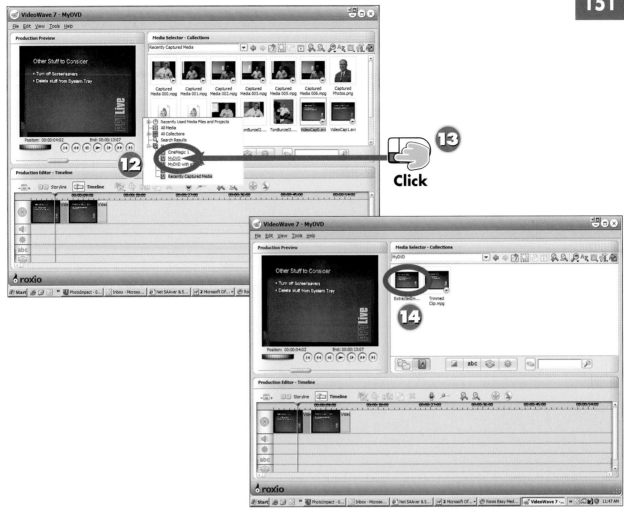

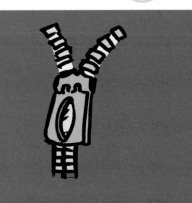

12. Find the collection that's been created for your named project.

13. Click the **Collection**.

14. Note the extracted frame is referenced in the Collection.

End

TIP

Adding the Image to Other Collections
While the extracted frame is referenced in the Collection named for the project, it can be added to any other Collection by using the **Add to Collection** button.

Creating a Slideshow from Images

Start

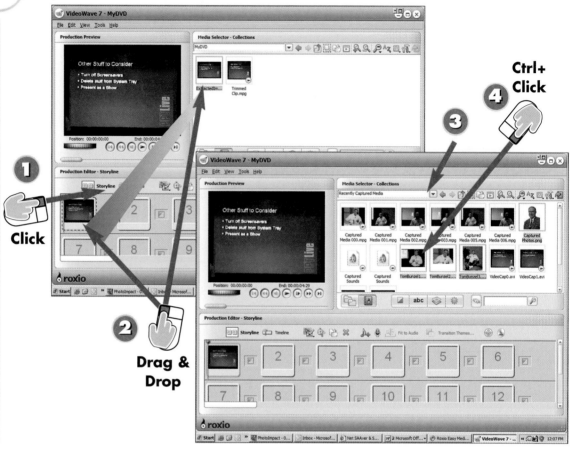

Ctrl+ Click

Click

Drag & Drop

1. Click to make sure you're in the **Storyline**.

2. Drag and drop the image you extracted, into the first Story segment.

3. Locate other images you want to use in other Collections.

4. **Ctrl+click** to select one or more images.

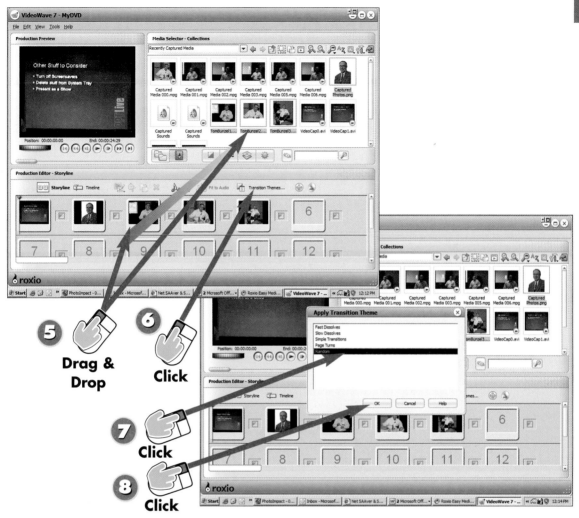

5. Drag and drop the selected images into the Storyline.

6. Click **Transition Themes**.

7. Select the **Random** transition theme.

8. Click **OK**. Accept the prompt to replace existing transitions.

See next page

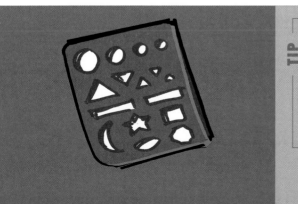

TIP

Changing Duration of the Images
You can click one or more images in the Storyline and click the **Adjust Duration** button change how long they appear in the slide show.

TIP

Change the Order of Images
To change the order that the images will appear on screen in your production, just drag and drop them to different slots in the Storyline, just as you would with videos.

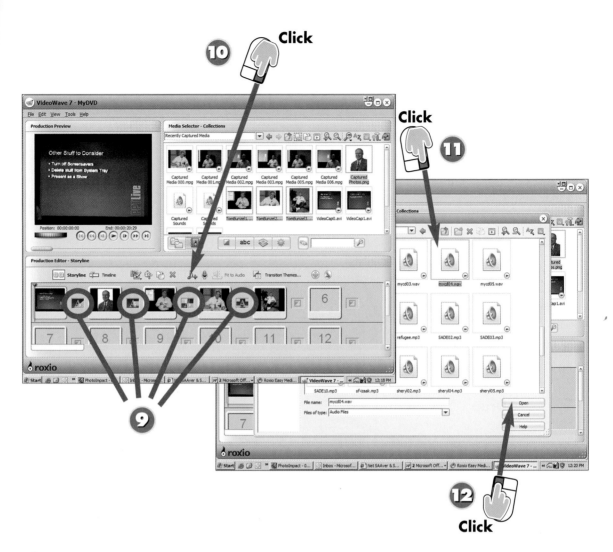

Click

Click

Click

(9) Note that transitions have been added.

(10) Click to **Add background audio to production**.

(11) Click an **audio** file to select it.

(12) Click **Open**.

Since a slide show by itself will have no audio, we'll combine it with a background audio file from our music library. See "Creating a Music Library" in Part 1 and "Creating a Music Collection in Nero" in Part 2.

Using Fit to Audio
If you have lots of slides and a short audio file you can click **Fit to Audio** to get them all in. With just a few slides, be careful, because Fit to Audio will increase their duration to expand to the length of the audio track.

Saving the SlideShow
You should save your slideshow production under a new name (like Slideshow) in your DVD video folder. Like your other newly outputted video files, you can use it in a DVD production or any program that uses Windows video files.

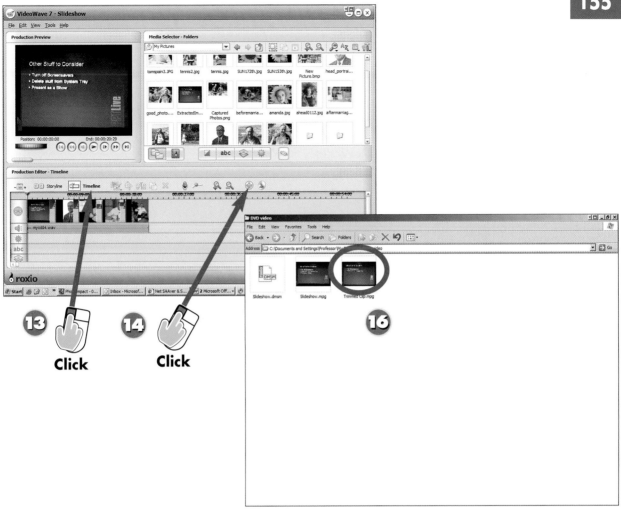

13 Click **Timeline** and note that the audio track has been added.

14 Click **Output your production in different formats**.

15 Complete the wizard as described earlier to create a new video file in the "Saving a Trimmed Clip" task.

16 Locate the completed file in your designated folder.

End

Using Create Slideshow from Home Page
If you click to **Create Slideshow** in the Roxio Home Page, you get an application called "Storyboard." It's exactly the same as VideoWave using the Storyline (instead of Timeline) view and will also open your previously saved slideshow productions.

Adding Narration
If you want to narrate a Slideshow (or any production) and have a microphone properly set up, click the little microphone icon to add a narrative track directly to your production.

Using Production Wizards

Start

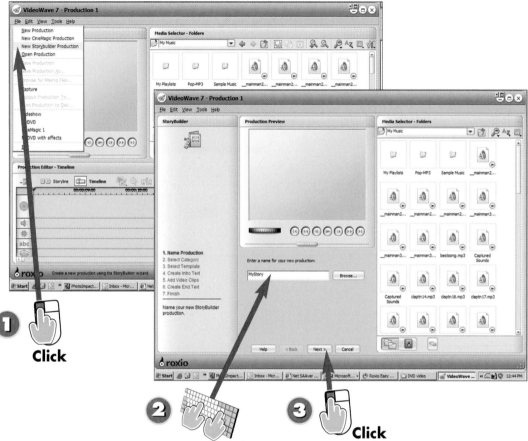

1 Click

2

3 Click

1 Click **File, New StoryBuilder Production**.

2 Type a name for your production.

3 Click **Next**.

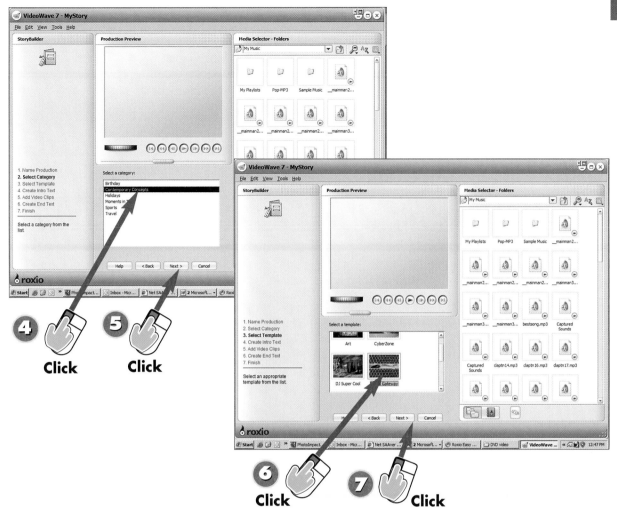

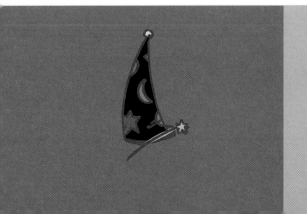

4 Click to select a **Category**.

5 Click **Next**.

6 Choose a **Theme**.

7 Click **Next**.

See next page

Customizing Project with CineMagic

You can experiment with CineMagic on your own by using your own music files as background audio for a more artistic video production.

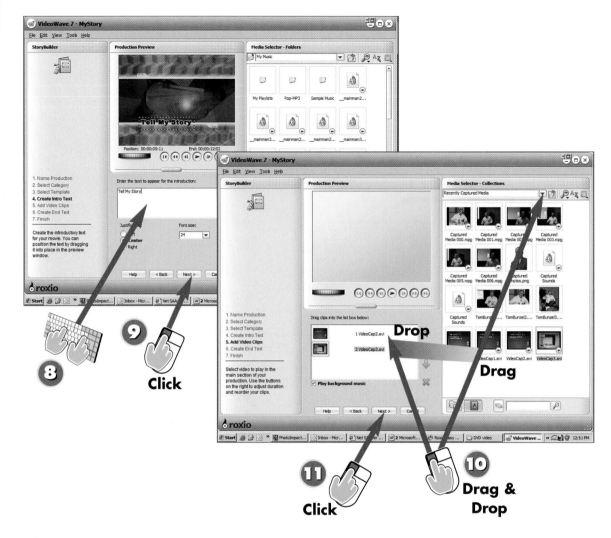

8 Type text to be used as an overlay for the introduction.

9 Click **Next**.

10 Open the Collection with your video clips and then drag and drop one or more clips into the production panel.

11 Click **Next**.

INTRODUCTION

We'll complete the StoryBuilder wizard by typing in some introductory text to overlay on the opening segment of the production and then choosing the clips that will play consecutively within the production.

TIP

Change the Clip Duration
Notice that there's a **Duration** button in this step of the wizard. You can click it to trim any selected clip to get rid of footage that you don't want to be included in the final production.

TIP

Keep the Audio Intact
Keep the **Play background music** box checked to maintain the audio that is part of the video files.

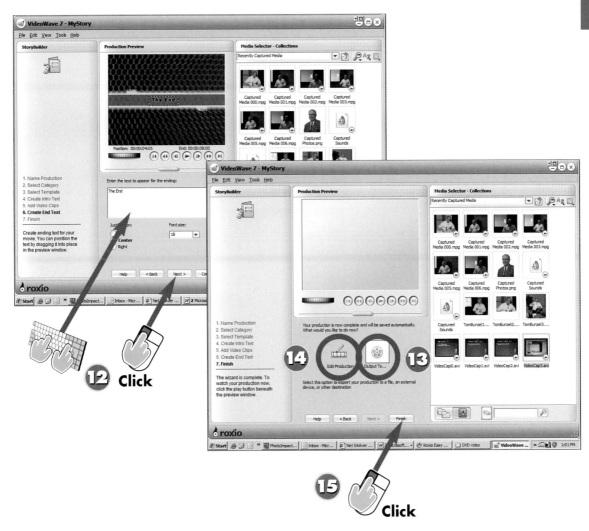

12 Type some ending text and click **Next**.

13 Use the **Output production** button to render a video file.

14 Use the **Edit Production** button to open it in VideoWave.

15 Click **Finish**.

End

TIP

Returning to VideoWave
By clicking **Edit Production** and then **Finish** you get the entire set of choices in the VideoWave Timeline. This lets you begin a production using the wizard and then complete it using the full features of VideoWave.

Adding Motion to Still Images

Start

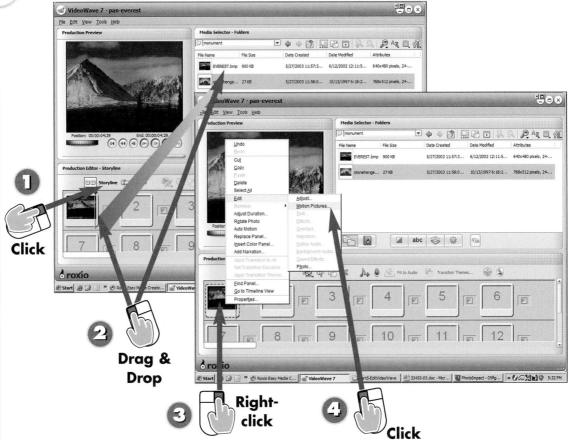

Click

Drag & Drop

Right-click

Click

1. Click to get into **Storyline** view.

2. Drag and drop a still image into a Story segment.

3. Right-click the image.

4. Click **Edit**, **Motion Picture**.

INTRODUCTION

One of the really neat tools that comes in VideoWave (or Storyboard, since it's for used specifically Slideshows) is the ability to add motion to a still image. Since his shows on PBS, this is sometimes known as the "Ken Burns effect."

TIP

Try AutoMotion First
Before going too far with the Motion Picture window, right-click the image first and select **AutoMotion**, which automatically applies a zoom-in effect to the selected image. You may find that the effect is just what you want.

HINT

Storyline vs. Timeline
You can access the Motion Picture effect from the Timeline as well, but for Slideshows and still images Storyline is probably a bit easier to use.

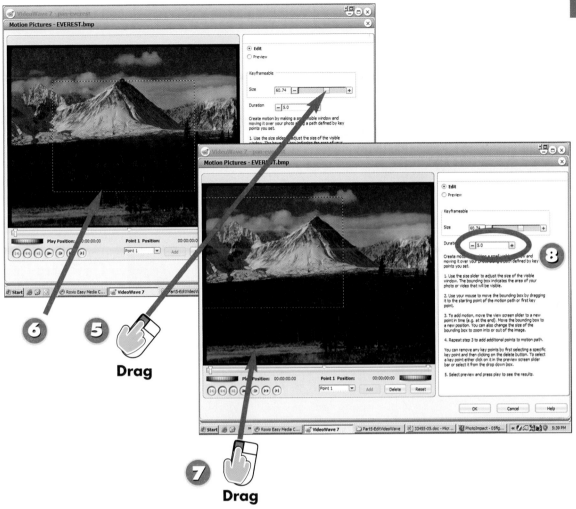

Drag

Drag

5 Drag the **Keyframeable slider** from + to –.

6 Watch how the window in the image is reduced.

7 Drag the **Keyframeable window** to the left edge of the image.

8 Check the **Duration** to see if it's enough time to accommodate the full movement of the effect, such as panning across the image.

See next page

What Is a Key Frame?

TIP

A key frame is a single point in the production where something changes dramatically, like the size or position of an object. (The first frame [Position 1] is always a key frame). Then, with a second key frame created and the object resized or moved, the program can automatically create the "in-between" frames to simulate motion.

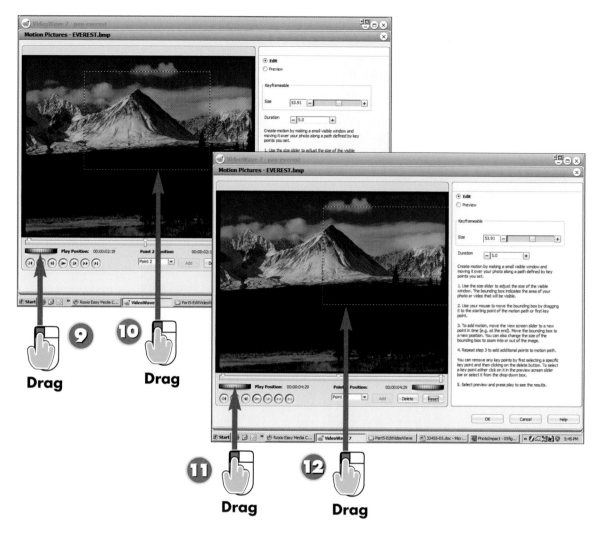

Drag **Drag**

Drag **Drag**

⑨ Drag the Play Position thumbwheel to advance the image to a point about halfway through the duration time that was set.

⑩ Move the Keyframeable window to a position halfway through the entire image. Note that this becomes the Point 2 position.

⑪ Drag the Play Position thumbwheel to the end of the clip.

⑫ Move the Keyframeable window to the right edge of the image. Note that this becomes the Point 3 position.

INTRODUCTION

What the Motion Pictures program does is enable you to determine what is seen at any point in time by repositioning or resizing the viewable area, and then the program will create the changes in the between frames. When it's all done, the segment will go back into your VideoWave production to be output to a new video file.

TIP

Follow the Motion Picture Hints
If you don't quite understand how to create a motion with keyframes, just follow the steps in the right panel of the Motion Picture window.

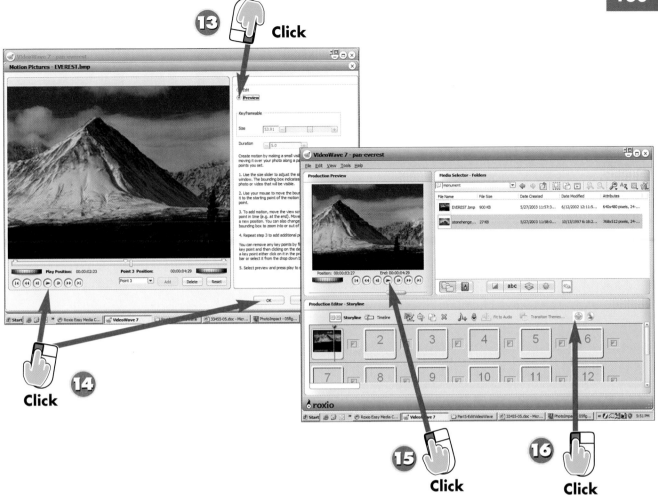

13 Click **Preview**.

14 Click the **Play** button to view the effect. Click **OK**.

15 Click the **Play** button to preview the entire production.

16 Click the **Output production** button to render a video file that you can use in your DVD project.

End

HINT
Image Distortion
The smaller you make the keyframeable window, the more motion you can achieve, but the more the image will need to be "stretched" to be full video size, resulting in some distortion.

TIP
Where to Preview
If you have just one image motion in your production, it makes no difference where you preview it, but the larger Motion Pictures preview in the window where you create the effect will show you any distortion more clearly. Use the Preview window in VideoWave to preview multiple story segments, such as a longer slideshow.

Creating a Project in DVD Builder

Now you're ready to assemble a DVD project that we will burn to a disc. The beauty of this format is that it plays on a consumer DVD player as well as a PC, and the user can navigate through the movies instantly using interactive menus, titles, and chapters.

When we played a DVD in Media Player at the end of Part 3, "Using Media Player to Enjoy CDs and DVDs," we saw the relationship between the menu, titles, and chapters. If you've rented a DVD movie you probably played it straight through as one long *title*. There may have been additional titles (segments) showing interviews, outtakes, and other features. If you wanted to locate a specific scene, you were able to locate *chapters* in the main title using the menu.

Using DVD Builder, you'll design the main menu with buttons, pictures, and text. The buttons will launch your titles or go deeper into longer titles and launch individual chapters.

DVD Builder lets you use predefined themes, which offer complementary backgrounds, buttons, and menus, or you can add your own backgrounds to the menus. Buttons can be lined up using an Auto Arrange button, or you can turn this feature off and move the elements of the menu where you want them. Font and text color formatting options familiar to users of other Windows graphics programs are also part of the application.

Designing an Interactive Menu in DVD Builder

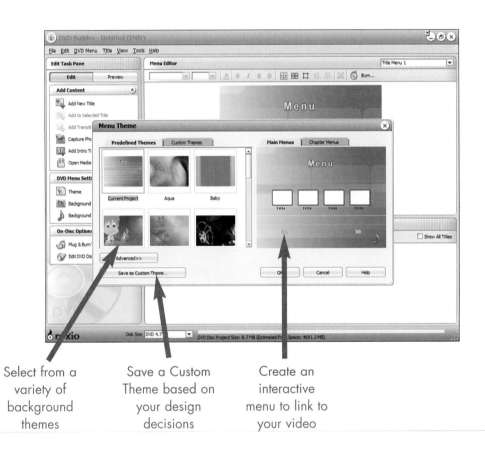

Select from a variety of background themes

Save a Custom Theme based on your design decisions

Create an interactive menu to link to your video

Starting Your DVD Production

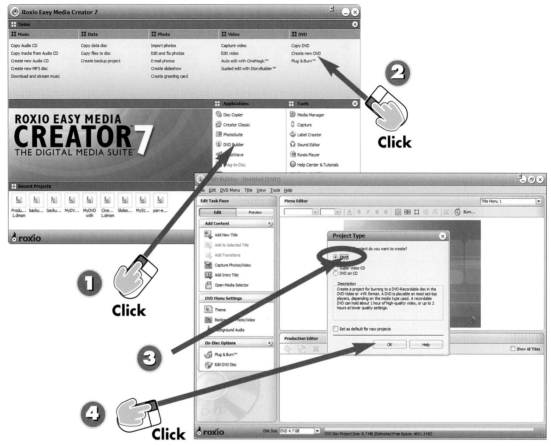

1 Click to open **DVD Builder**.

2 Or click to **Create New DVD**.

3 Leave the default project type as **DVD**.

4 Click **OK**.

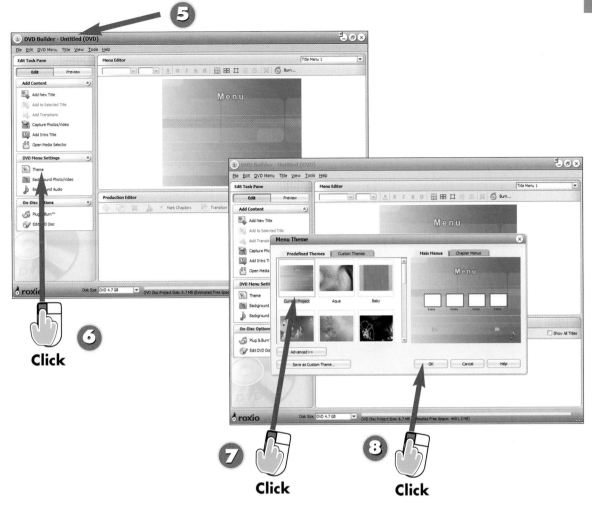

5 DVD Builder opens a new **Untitled** project. Your opening menu is available to edit.

6 Click **Theme**. Drag through the **Predefined Themes** to see other options.

7 Click the **Current Project** theme.

8 Click **OK**. You are now ready for the next task—adding a title.

End

Launch from VideoWave
You can also open DVD Builder by clicking the disc icon in VideoWave next to the **Output to other formats** button.

Using Other Themes
Notice how applying a new theme changes the look of not just the background, but the frames of the buttons and the design and color of the text. A theme provides a completely different feel and flavor for your project.

Video CDs
Video CDs and Super Video CDs are movie discs with slightly less interactivity than DVDs but they play nearly everywhere. SVCDs hold less video because the video is better quality—MPEG-2. VCDs hold more video of VHS quality.

Adding a Title to the DVD Project

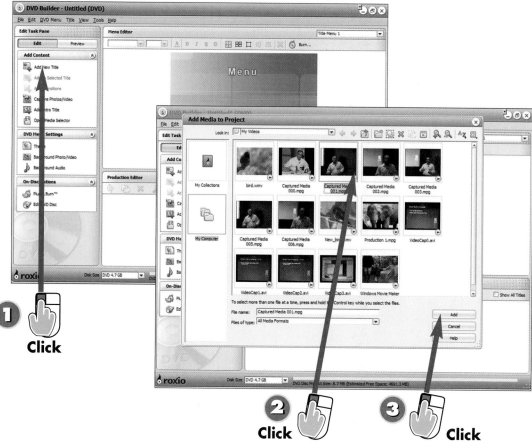

Click

Click

Click

1 Click **Add New Title**.

2 Click to select a Title video.

3 Click **Add**.

INTRODUCTION

Titles are the main segments of your DVD, for which you'll be using the final video files you output from VideoWave in Part 5. By adding them to the menu, you create links that users can click to watch the videos in whatever order that they want.

TIP

Finding the Right Video
Remember where you saved your video output files. You can locate them using the Folders or Collections view. To add a collection to the project, click **My Collections** in the Add Media to Project window.

HINT

Slideshows and Still Images
You can also include slideshows and still images in the Production Editor as DVD titles. You can import a slideshow production that was saved in VideoWave (or StoryBoard) as a new title.

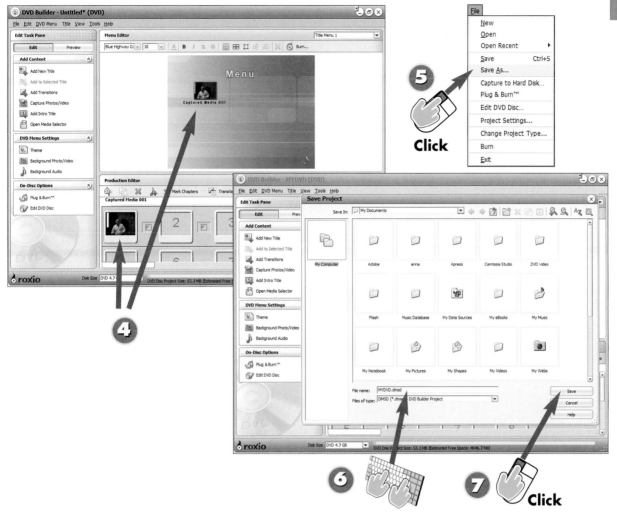

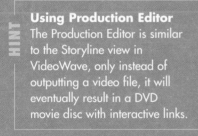

4 The Title link is added to the menu and the title is added to the Production Editor.

5 Click **File**, **Save As**.

6 Name your new DVD project.

7 Click **Save**.

End

Adding More Titles and Transitions

Start

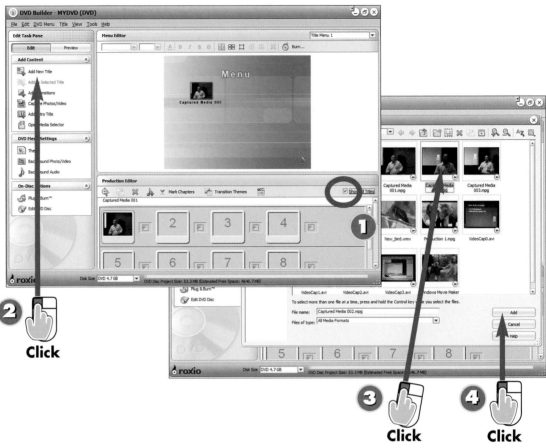

Click **Click**

Click

① Make sure **Show All Titles** is checked.

② Click **Add New Title**.

③ Click to select the video file to be your next title.

④ Click **Add**.

TIP

Why Add Titles?
Each title will return to the current menu (in this case the main menu) when it finishes. As you'll see in this task, you can also click **Add to Selected Title** to make a title that consists of more than one video, with transitions in between.

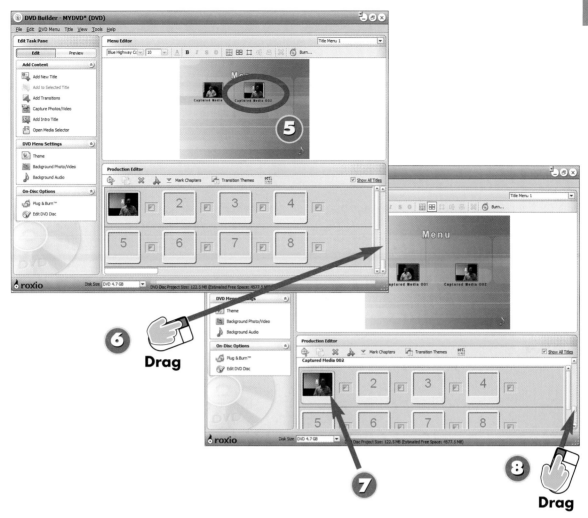

Drag

Drag

⑤ Notice that a second button has been added to the menu.

⑥ Drag the scrollbar on the outside of the Production Editor.

⑦ A second title has been started with the selected clip in first position.

⑧ Drag the scroll bar back up the outside of the Production Editor until you see the first title you added to the project.

See next page

Why Two Scrollbars?
The outside scrollbar moves between titles. The inside scrollbar will move within a title, which will help if you add more video or images to a given title.

Moving the Buttons
When the titles are first added, they go into the center of the menu. As we'll see in "Redesigning Your Menus," if you deselect the **Autoarrange** button you can drag your buttons anywhere you want them within the menu.

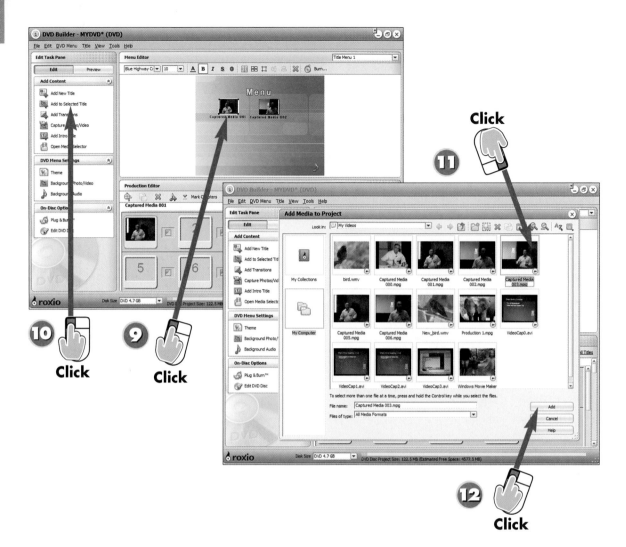

9   Click the button for the first title.

10   Click **Add to Selected Title**.

11   Click to select another video or image to add to the first title.

12   Click **Add**. The clip is added to the first title.

Now you can continue to arrange your titles on the menu, and also add video clips and still images to existing titles. A nice feature is putting transitions between portions of a title, which give it a broadcast-type of feel.

TIP

Adding to a Title
The empty placeholders represent slots for adding additional video or images to a title. To add to a title, you can right-click a blank placeholder and select **Insert Video/Photo**.

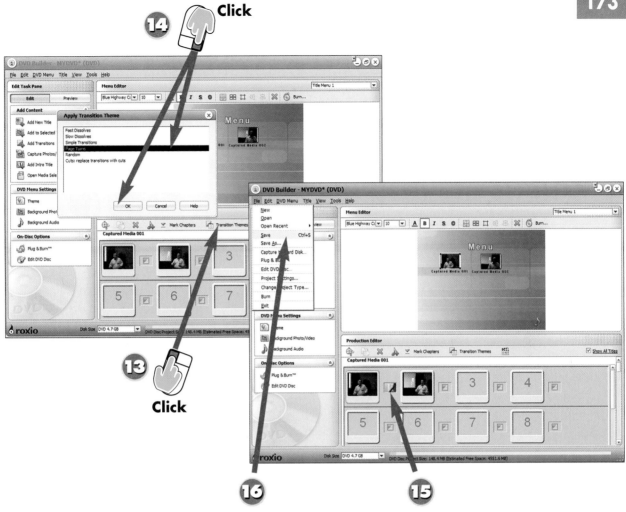

Click

Click

13 Click **Transition Themes**.

14 Click **Page Turns** and **OK**.

15 A transition is added between the clips in the first title.

16 Click **File**, **Save** to save the project so far.

End

Doing a Sneak Preview

Start

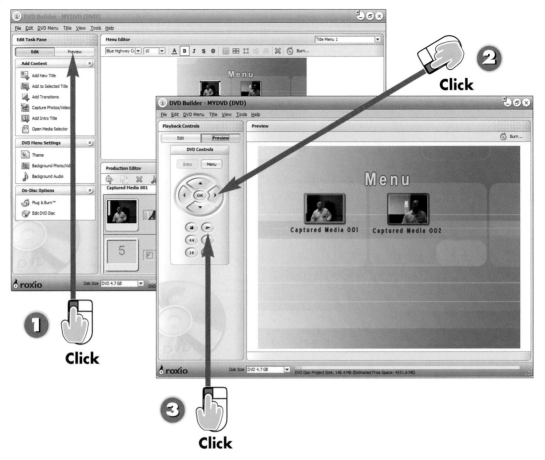

Click ②

Click ①

Click ③

① With your project open in DVD Builder, click **Preview**.

② Click to advance through your titles.

③ Click **Play**.

INTRODUCTION

Normally you might not preview the project until you've added more content, but to see the difference between your titles and get a sense of where we're going, let's do a *sneak preview*. We'll cover preview and burning in more detail in the next part.

TIP

Selecting Titles to Play
Many remote controls on DVD players will let you click on a title and then click Play. In the Preview window, however, you need to use the simulated remote control to highlight a title to play.

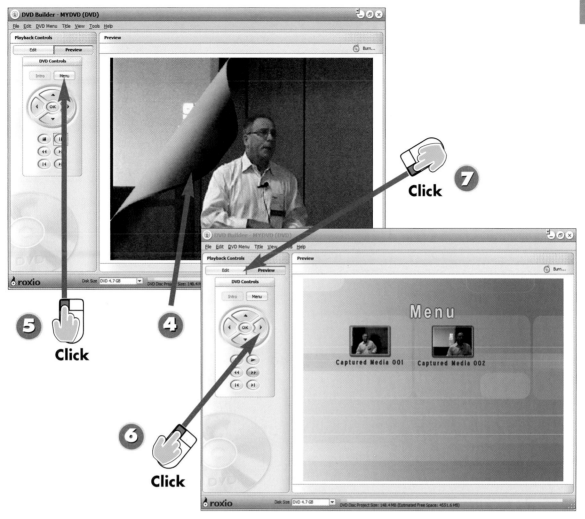

4 Watch the title with the Page Turn transition.

5 You can wait until the title finishes or click **Menu**.

6 You can select and play the other title.

7 Click **Edit** to return to DVD Builder's Production Editor.

End

Turn Off the Music
DVD Builder's themes play
music with menus by default.
For your sanity you might want
to click **DVD Menu**, **Remove
Background Audio**.

Add Background Audio
If you have a favorite music clip
or narration to accompany the
menu, just click **Background
Audio** under DVD Menu
Settings to substitute yours for
the music provided with the
theme.

Adding Chapters

Start

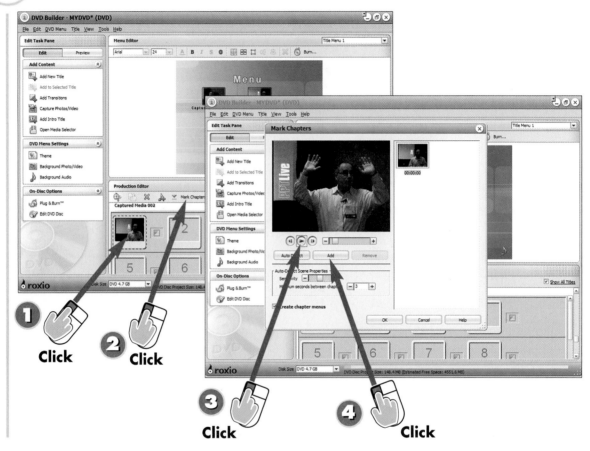

Click ① **Click** ② **Click** ③ **Click** ④

① In the Production Editor, click the title in which you want to create chapters.

② Click **Mark Chapters**.

③ Click **Play** to play the clip to a point you want to break out as a chapter.

④ Click **Add**.

INTRODUCTION

You may want to insert some markers in a longer title to enable users to jump directly to a specific segment within the longer video. You've probably seen this in rented movie DVDs where you can move through the entire film by *chapters* to find a favorite scene or skip past stuff that may be boring.

TIP

Finding Chapter Points
You can also drag through the clip using the scrollbar to locate a chapter point visually. If the clip was captured in DV, **Auto Detect** will find breaks in the subject matter and create chapters for you.

TIP

Deleting Chapter Points
You can select any chapter point (except the opening frame) in the **Mark Chapters** window and click **Remove**.

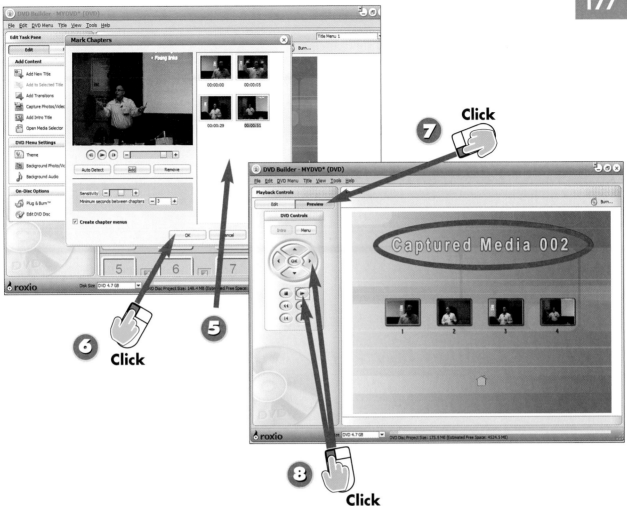

5 Your chapters appear in the right panel.

6 Click **OK**.

7 Click **Preview**.

8 Click the **selector** to locate the title that now contains chapters, then click **Play**. The chapter menu appears.

End

Numbered Segments
The chapter menu shows the segments in a numbered sequence. As you can see in step 8, the chapter menu heading is the same as the caption on the button for the title, which we'll edit in the next task.

Themes for Chapter Menus
Chapter menus will reflect the theme choices you make for the menu that launches them, in this case the current menu. We'll see how to change them in the **Menu Theme** window later in this chapter in the section called "Redesigning Your Menus."

Editing the Menu Text

Start

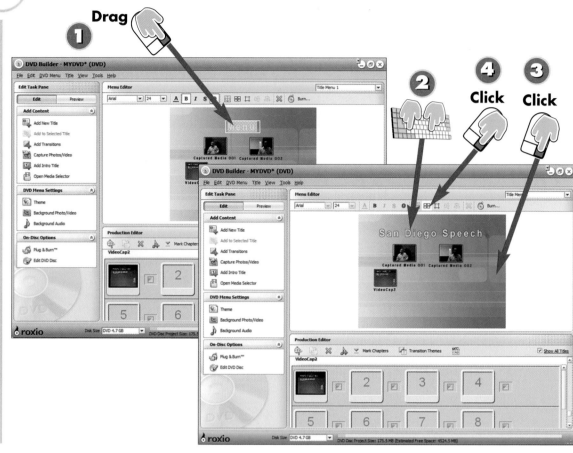

Drag

Click **Click**

1 Click and drag to select the placeholder for Main Menu text.

2 Type a new heading for the Main Menu ("San Diego Speech").

3 Click elsewhere to deselect the new text.

4 Click **Autoarrange**. Autoarrange lines up your buttons on an invisible grid.

So far the menu you've created has a predefined background design, but the text is probably not what you want, and you might also want to change the layout and design before burning the disc.

TIP

Deselect Autoarrange
If you want to drag and move buttons around the menu and can't, deselect **Autoarrange** and you can manually move the objects. If you click Autoarrange again, whatever objects you've created on the menu are lined up in a grid.

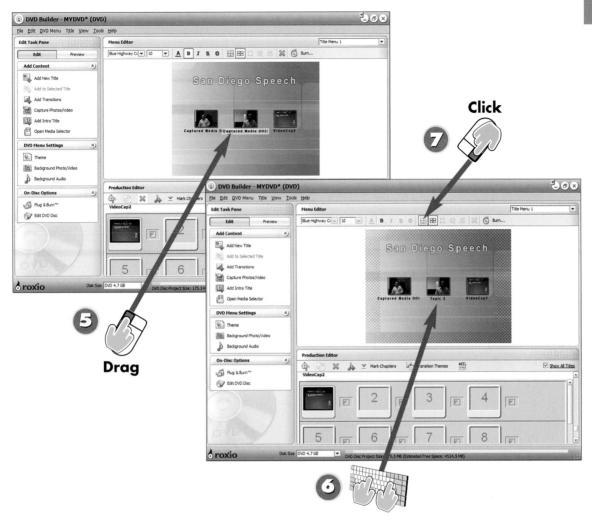

Click

Drag

5 Click and drag to select a title caption.

6 Type in a new caption.

7 Click to select the **TV Safe Zone** to make sure your project is all visible within the limits of a TV's viewing screen.

End

What's the TV Safe Zone?
If your DVD is shown on a consumer DVD player, some displays will cut off the edges. The TV Safe Zone provides a guide as to what should display on all monitors, even smaller screens.

Captions on the Chapter Menu
By default the captions under the buttons are the file names of the titles. When you change the caption for the button leading to a title broken into chapters, the caption for the title button ("Topic 2", here) will be reflected on the heading for the chapter menu.

Redesigning Your Menus

Start

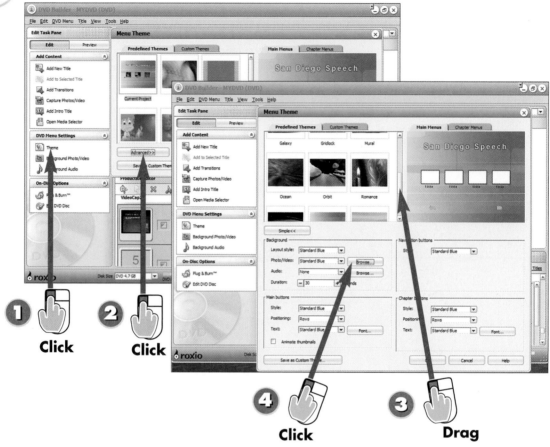

1 Click

2 Click

4 Click

3 Drag

1 Click **Theme** in the DVD Menu Settings.

2 Click **Advanced** in the Menu Theme Window.

3 Drag the scrollbar to see other layouts you can apply from **Layout Style**.

4 Click **Browse** to add a background photo.

INTRODUCTION

So far the menu design is based on the specific theme you accepted earlier. As you will now see, all of your design options are based on changing predefined themes and saving them as a custom theme.

HINT

Layouts and Themes
The Layout Styles in the Background area reflect the gallery of predefined themes. Choosing a predefined theme selects a background layout and vice versa.

HINT

Adding a Background Video
Note that you can browse for a photo/video for the background. Selecting a video may make the menu hard to look at so if you try this feature, preview it to see if it works for you before you burn it to a DVD.

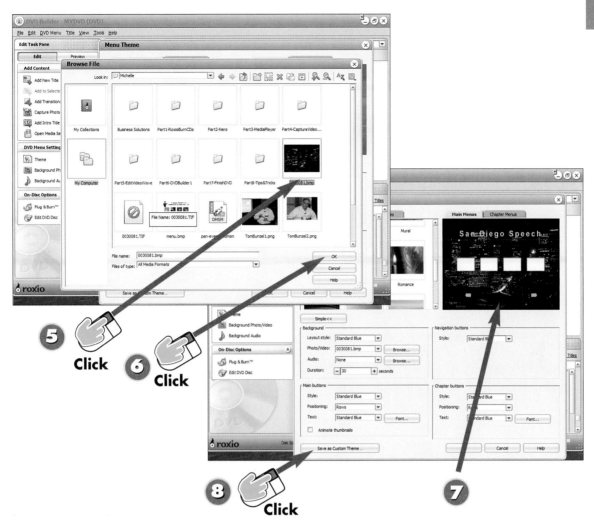

5 Click to select a new background photo.

6 Click **OK**.

7 Your background photo is set in the menu.

8 Click **Save as Custom Theme**.

See next page

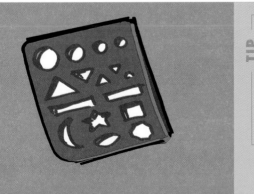

Setting Other Options
Besides the background photo, experiment with the other styles you can change for the buttons on the main menu and chapter menu. All of the changes can be saved as a custom theme.

TIP

9 Type a name for the theme ("CityScape").

10 Click **OK**.

11 Click the **Custom Themes** tab.

12 Your saved **custom theme** is now available for other projects.

Once you've modified a theme with the look exactly the way you want, you will want to save it so you can reapply those same stylistic elements again to another project. Your newly named theme will be available under the Custom Themes tab.

Changing a Custom Theme

To change elements of your custom theme, just type in the same name when you chose to save it, and the new choices will overwrite the old ones.

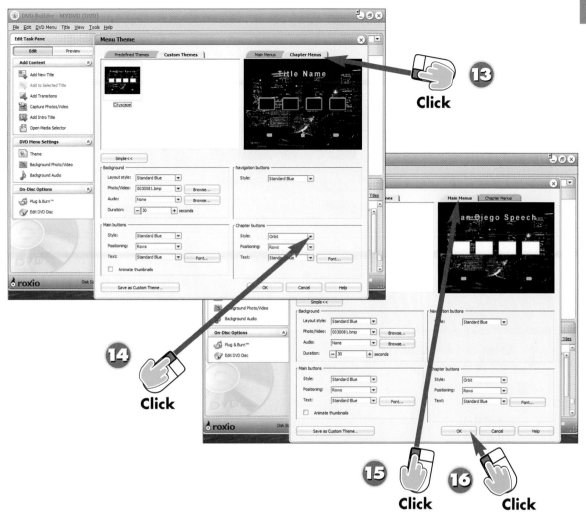

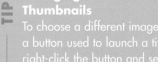

13 Click **Chapter Menus**.

14 Click to change the **button style**. Watch the buttons change their look in the Chapter menu.

15 Click the **Main Menus** tab again. Continue to change styles for the main menu.

16 Click **OK** to return to the Production Editor.

End

TIP

Changing Button Thumbnails
To choose a different image of a button used to launch a title, right-click the button and select **Change Thumbnail**.

HINT

Animating Thumbnails
Be careful about checking the Animate Thumbnails box, because you won't see the results in the preview window, and it may be quite jarring to the viewer. Animated thumbnails are only available if the recording format is DVD-video.

Adding an Intro Title

Start

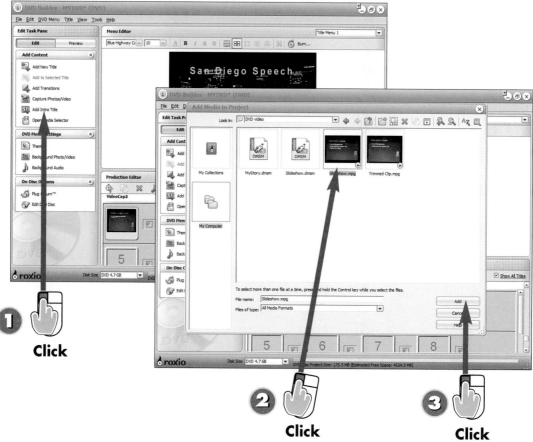

1 Click
2 Click
3 Click

1 Click **Add Intro Title**.

2 Select the Slideshow (or video).

3 Click **Add**.

TIP

Returning to StoryBoard
Clicking the **movie scene-marker** icon in the Production Editor will bring you back to StoryBoard, which is the Storyline view of VideoWave. As you saw in Part 5, that's where you can edit and re-output your videos and slideshows.

HINT

Using the Project Files
Notice that you can add the *project files* you created in VideoWave to DVD Builder, but you will find that when it's time to burn the disc, these will still need to be converted to video. Using the final output video, if you've created it, is faster.

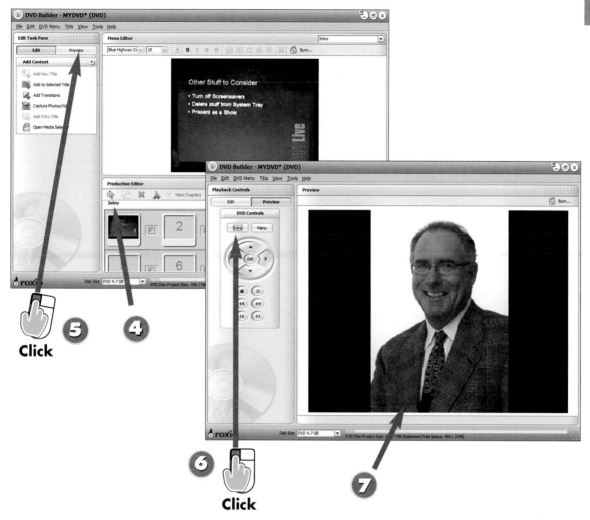

Click ⑤ ④

⑥ **Click**

⑦

④ Your intro video goes to the top of the Production Editor.

⑤ Click **Preview**.

⑥ Click **Intro**.

⑦ Watch the **Intro Video** or Slideshow.

End

Menus and Intro Drop List
You can select to view the menus or intros from a drop-down list in the upper right of DVD Builder's main window. This will let you instantly access any of the menus or the intro title for revision, but it won't let you manually revise the chapter menus.

Creating a Final DVD Movie Disc

If you've been working through the book's previous tasks, at this point you should have a complete project in your Production Editor in DVD Builder. If not, you'll want to look back to Parts 5 and 6 to get a project ready to burn to DVD.

The project will probably consist of several titles, transitions between clips within your titles, and perhaps chapters within longer title segments. We'll do a final preview before going through the burn process, and perhaps you'll find it helpful (as we did) to return to the DVD Builder to change some elements in your production.

As we prepare to burn, we'll examine some of the final settings to ensure that our project will record properly and that all of our video will fit onto a DVD disc. As we saw with audio CDs, there is also an option for burning a disc image, which will enable you to reproduce the finished project as many times as you like.

And at the end of the chapter you'll also see how to edit a DVD on a rewritable DVD disc, and burn directly from your DV camcorder to create a new DVD without using DVD Builder at all.

In Preview, We Finalize Our Project and Begin to Burn

Select a title to Preview

Burn to DVD

Play your Titles

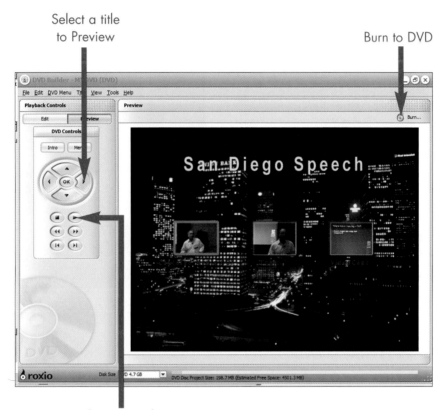

Doing a Final Preview

Start

Click ①

Click ②

Click ③

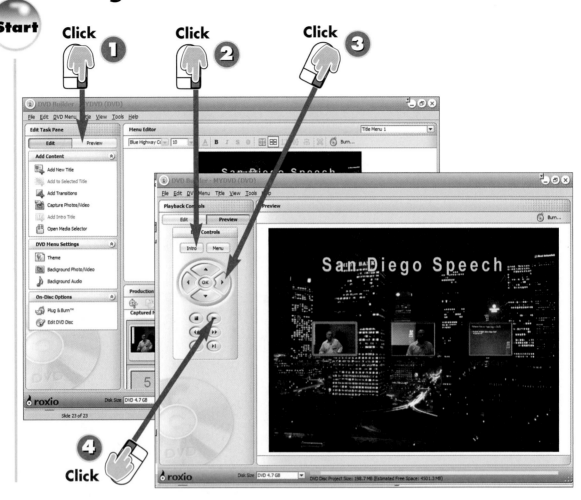

Click ④

① Click **Preview** in DVD Builder.

② Click **Intro** to watch your opening video.

③ Click to select a title to check.

④ Click **Play** to play the selected title.

It's important to know that when you burn discs, there will be no surprises. Maybe the wrong music will play with a menu, or a link might take us somewhere we did not expect. Doing a thorough preview will help avoid these problems.

Rearranging Your Titles
One of the things to watch for in Preview is whether your titles make sense in the order or on the menus where they appear. Your Production Editor is your storyboard for the project, and your Preview window is your last chance to see whether it works.

Returning to the Menu
While a clip is playing in Preview, you can always click Menu to return to its menu. If you're previewing a chapter, it will return to the chapter menu.

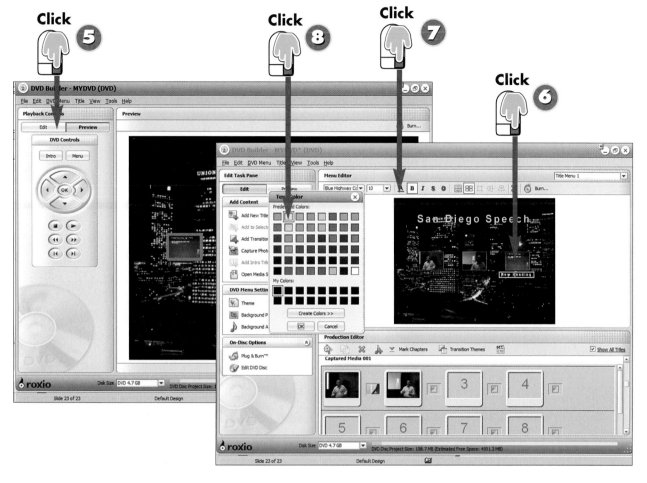

5 If you find that there's a chapter menu that needs a new heading, click **Edit** to return to the Production Editor.

6 Select a caption to change its text color by dragging through the text.

7 Click the **Text Color** button.

8 Click a swatch to select a new color for the caption.

End

Changing Durations
If you worked through the tasks on VideoWave, you'll remember that we changed the duration of our clips there. However, notice that there is a Duration button in the Production Editor as well to let you make last-minute changes after you preview.

Burning the Project

Start

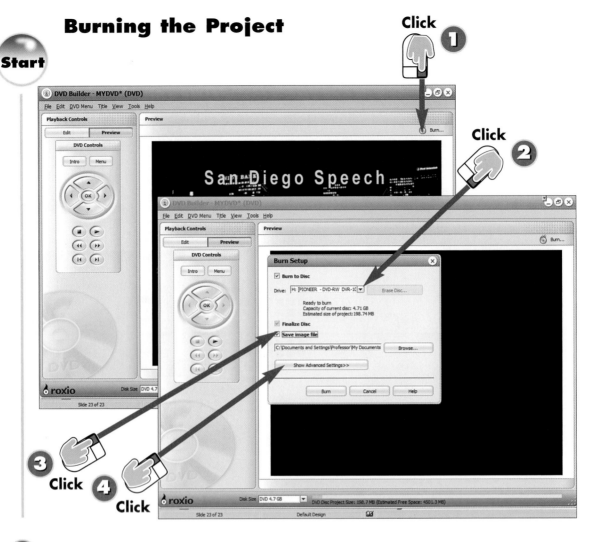

Click **1**

Click **2**

Click **3**

Click **4**

Click

1 Click **Burn**.

2 Click to select the destination drive.

3 Choose to **Save Image File** if you want.

4 Click **Show Advanced Settings**.

While there is a Burn button in the Production Editor, let's assume we've finished a final preview and decided to burn our disc. We need to put a blank DVD into our recordable drive. As we saw when we burned audio and data CDs, there are important options to review—in the case of DVDs these will involve the quality settings of the video to be burned, so that the capacity of the disc isn't exceeded, and whether to save a disc image file.

Saving a Disc Image
As you saw in Creator Classic (Part 1, "Creating CDs with Creator Classic in Easy Media Creator"), an image file will let you reproduce a project as many times as you want. Bear in mind that a DVD image file may be enormous, so make sure you keep track of available disk space.

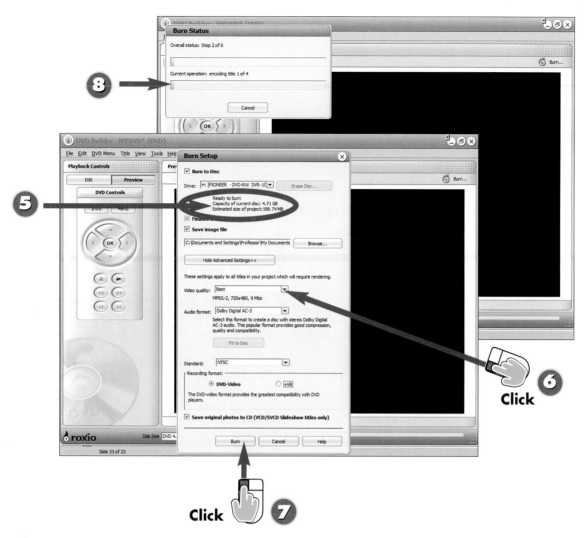

Click

Click

5 Make sure there is enough room on the disc for your project.

6 If you need room on the disc, reduce video quality.

7 Click **Burn**.

8 Watch the progress in the Burn Status dialog as DVD Builder burns your project.

End

It Takes Time to Burn the Disc
Burning a DVD is generally a two step process, because some of the video will need to be *encoded* into the MPEG-2 format before the disc is finally burned. If you have a lot of video and an older burner, take the rest of the day off. For a small project with a newer (8X or higher) burner, and the right media, lunch might be long enough.

Finalize Disc
The Finalize Disc option is set by default for DVD projects because discs that remain open for additional data will not play in many DVD players.

Using On-Disc Options

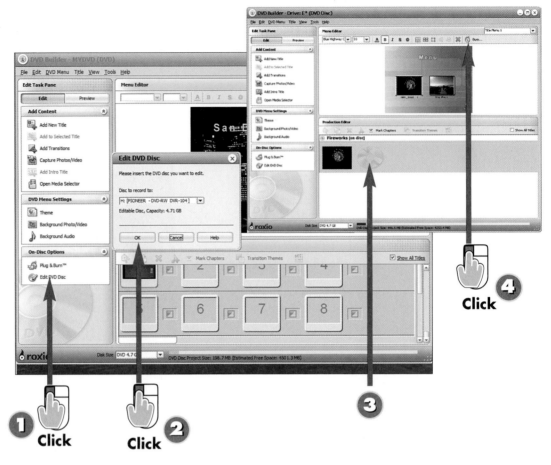

Click

Click

Click

1️⃣ Click **Edit DVD Disc**.

2️⃣ Access the burner with the DVD disc you want to revise. Click **OK**.

3️⃣ DVD Builder opens (see Part 6 for how to use DVD Builder). Delete or add titles in the Production Editor.

4️⃣ Click **Burn**.

DVD Builder lets you re-edit some DVD discs and also burn a disc automatically from a DV source after capturing your segments in a Plug & Burn wizard.

Using the Right Media
If you are burning or editing on-disc, you should use rewritable media. Write-once media won't work. Make sure you use either "-RW" or "+RW" discs.

Marking Chapters
If your media is readable to Edit DVD, you should be able to add new chapters to a title as well. Because you have the full power of the DVD Builder program, you can click the **Mark Chapters** button to open any title and add new chapters to it.

Click

5

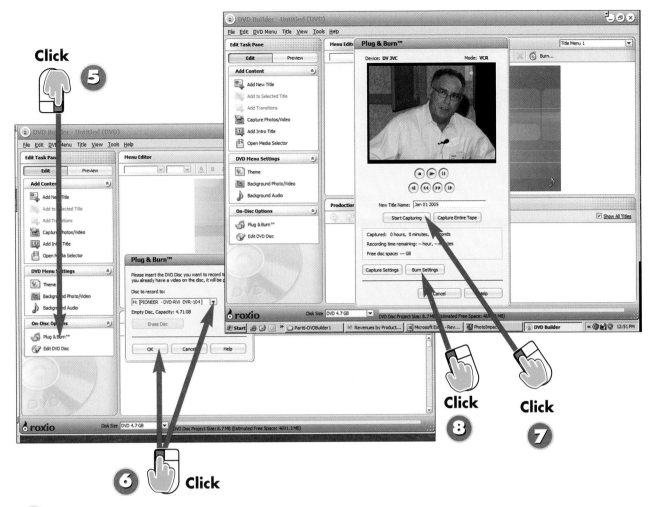

Click

8

Click

7

6 **Click**

5 Click **Plug & Burn**.

6 Select the burner with a blank DVD. Plug in your DV camcorder, turn it on to VTR mode, and click **OK**.

7 Locate the segments to capture. Click **Start Capturing**.

8 When the footage is captured, click **Burn Settings** and complete burning the disc.

End

Capturing an Entire Tape
Click **Plug & Burn** under On-Disc Options to capture one entire DV tape automatically before burning it to disc.

Tips and Techniques

We've come a long way in our description of different ways to create and burn CD and DVD projects. By now you probably realize that each project is only as good as its source material. In our chapter on VideoWave, we covered the Capture window as the essential part of Easy Media Creator for getting and editing source video.

In this final chapter, we want to take a look at other techniques for working with images and sound as potential source material for your projects. Along the way we'll take a quick look at two other parts of Easy Media Creator 7: PhotoSuite 7 and Sound Editor.

While you may already be familiar with an image editing program (such as Adobe Photoshop or Photoshop Elements), it's nice to know that Easy Media Creator also has an image editing program that integrates with the other components of the suite. If you like the way that you can open projects from the bottom of the Easy Media Creator home page, then using PhotoSuite may be appealing to you, so we've got a couple of tasks here to introduce you to the program.

Another component of Easy Media Creator that you should know about is the Sound Editor, which gives you a lot of control over digital audio files. We'll show you how to capture audio into Sound Editor and then do a few short tasks to get you more comfortable with the tool.

Sound Editor

Save the files in a format you can use in a CD or DVD

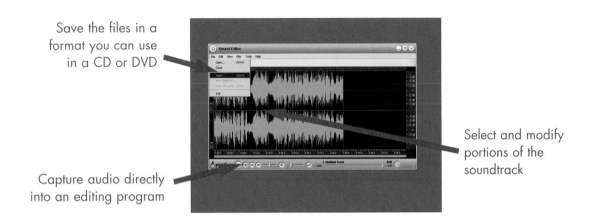

Select and modify portions of the soundtrack

Capture audio directly into an editing program

PhotoSuite

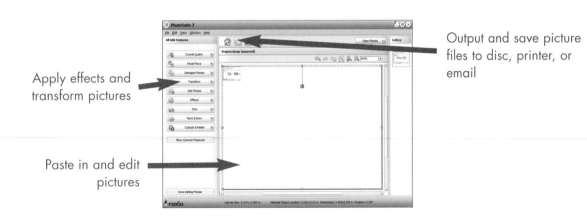

Output and save picture files to disc, printer, or email

Apply effects and transform pictures

Paste in and edit pictures

Grabbing Screenshots from Other Programs

Start

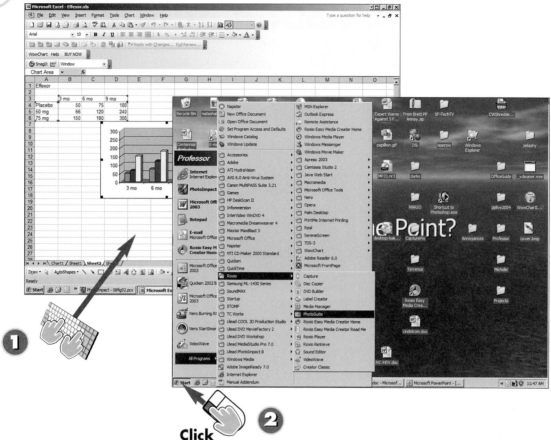

Click ... **2**

1 With the image on screen, press the **PrintScrn** key on your keyboard.

2 Click **Start**, **All Programs**, **Roxio**, **PhotoSuite 7**.

We've already seen the effectiveness of using an image in a slideshow or as a background for a menu. What if you need an image quickly from a program that doesn't necessarily save or *export* files as images, like Microsoft Excel? For example, one area where you might use a DVD with a chart is a business presentation that has other video, but you also need to show financial information.

TIP

Working with Images
You can use other image editors to do what we're doing, but we want to use a tool that's included in Easy Media Creator.

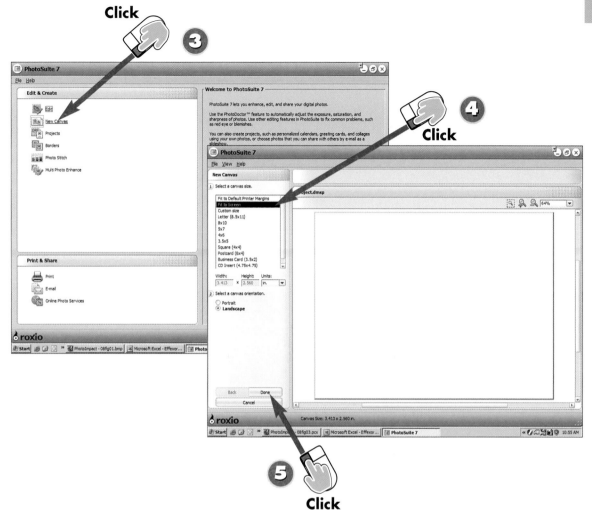

Click

Click

Click

3 Click **New Canvas** in PhotoSuite 7.

4 Click **Fit to Screen**.

5 Click **Done**.

See next page

Editing with PhotoSuite 7
You can also use PhotoSuite 7 to open an image file, such as the one we captured from a digital camera or scanner (in Part 4, "Acquiring Still Images," **p.116**). In the next task we'll see how to crop an image using this program.

Click 6

Drag 7

8 Drag

9 Drag

6 Click **Edit**, **Paste** on the main menu.

7 The screen you captured appears as a small icon.

8 Drag the image into a corner.

9 Drag out the lower-right corner of the image to stretch it across the entire canvas.

Once you've opened PhotoSuite to create a new image file from the screenshot, you'll need to paste it in and do a bit of manipulation. Finally you'll save the file in a format that enables you to use it in VideoWave or StoryBoard.

Other PhotoSuite Options
Notice that besides **Fit to Screen**, you can create compositions in PhotoSuite for other sizes and applications. If you click the **Custom** option, you can create your own dimensions.

Clipboard Limitations
Microsoft Office Applications can fit up to 24 items on the Office clipboard. PhotoSuite uses the Windows clipboard but is limited to storing only one object at a time. Make sure you don't copy anything else until after you paste your object into PhotoSuite.

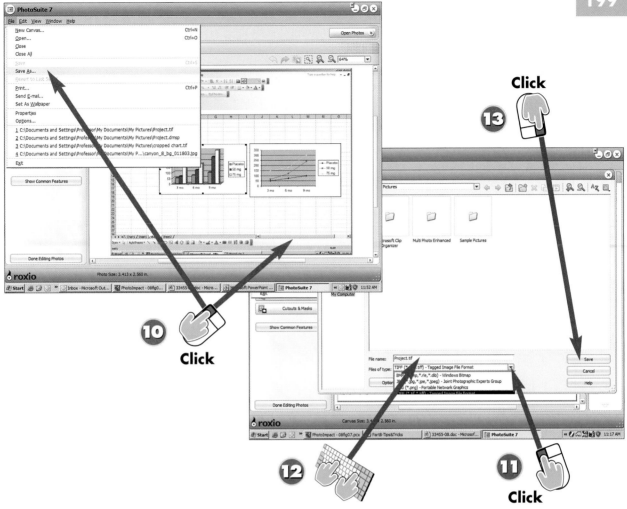

10 Your image now fills out PhotoSuite's editing window. Click **File**, **Save As**.

11 Click to change the **File Type** to an image file, like TIF.

12 Name the file.

13 Click **Save**.

End

Using the Image
With the image saved you can add it directly to a VideoWave or DVD Builder project or use it in collections.

Using Alt+PrintScn
In step 1, if you want to capture just the chart without needing the entire Excel worksheet, right-click the chart and choose **Chart Window**. Then use **Alt+PrintScn** to capture only the chart.

Location, Location, Location
Make sure you save the image to a folder you will remember, or use the Collections option to keep track of the file wherever it is saved.

Cropping an Image in PhotoSuite 7

Start

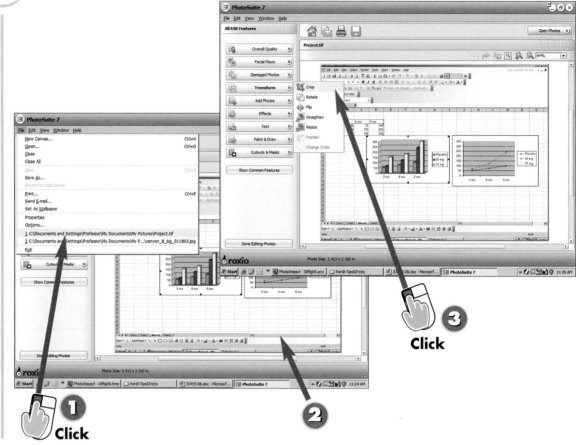

Click ①

Click ②

Click ③

① Click **File**, *Your Saved File's Name* to reopen your image or open another similar file to work on.

② The full screen you captured earlier is in the canvas.

③ Click **Transform**, **Crop**.

Sometimes you have captured an image from a digital camera or scanner, or grabbed a computer screen, and you don't necessarily want to use the whole image. Just as we trimmed video in VideoWave, we can crop images in PhotoSuite 7.

Image Editors Vary

TIP

In many image editors you would first select an area of the image, and then use a tool like Crop. PhotoSuite works a bit differently in having you define the goal or effect first, and then giving you the selection to work with.

Click

4

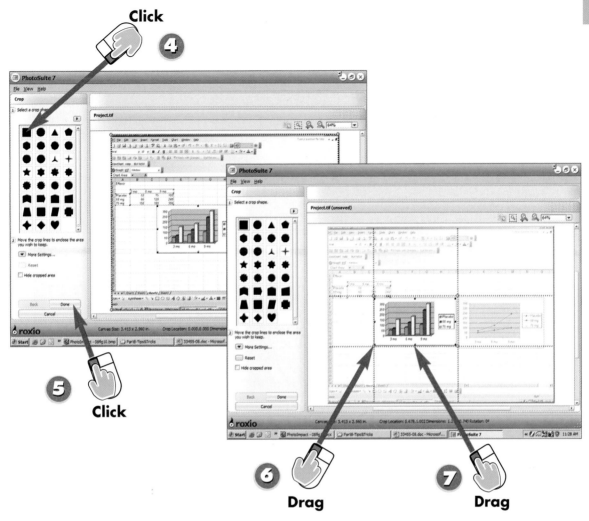

5 **Click**

6 **Drag**

7 **Drag**

4 Click the **Rectangle** crop shape.

5 Click **Done.**

6 Drag in the corners of the rectangle around the cropped area.

7 Drag in the borders around the cropped area.

See next page

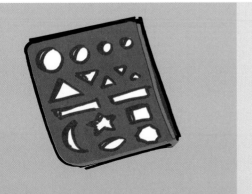

Other Cropping Shapes
There is an entire gallery of cropping shapes to use for different effects with your images. Experiment with these shapes as special effects besides the ordinary rectangular crop, and if you don't like the results, use **Edit**, **Undo**.

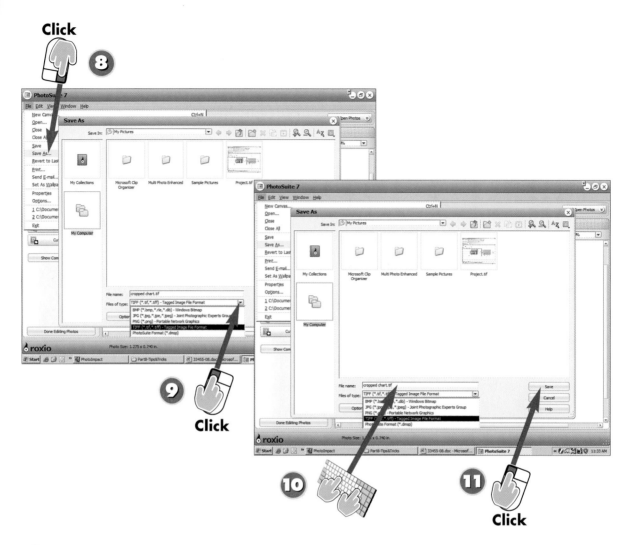

8 Click **File**, **Save As** on the main menu.

9 Click to select an **Image Format**.

10 Rename your file to create a new image instead of overwriting the one you opened.

11 Click **Save**.

Now that we've saved the image we grabbed from another program, let's continue to work with it in a more familiar program—VideoWave. First we'll save it as a new image file, and then use it in a slide show.

Using the Image in Other Programs

You can use the PhotoSuite 7 image in other programs for different purposes. For any other program, check the file types that it accepts and select the correct file type after you choose **File**, **Save As** in PhotoSuite.

Using the Image Online

If the ultimate destination of the image is to go into a web page, choose a JPG, GIF, or PNG in step 10. We've kept it as a TIF file because it remains uncompressed, preserving as much of its quality as possible.

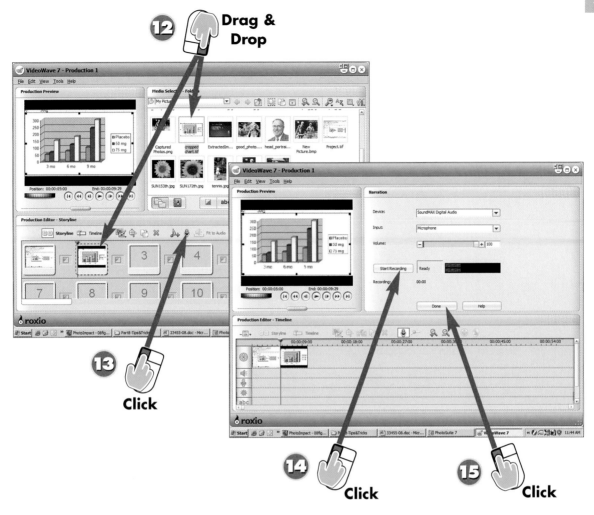

12 Locate the cropped file in VideoWave by opening folder where you saved it and drag it into the project.

13 Click **Add Narration**.

14 Click **Start Recording** narration through a microphone.

15 Click **Done**.

Using Narration
To use Narration you will need to have a microphone properly set up on your Windows XP computer. When the segment is recorded and you click **Done**, and the narration is added to the timeline in conjunction with the image.

Working with Sound
Later in this chapter we will cover other ways to acquire audio from LPs, cassettes, and other analog sources. See "Capturing Music from LPs or Cassettes," **p.208** and "Recording into Sound Editor," **p.212**.

Image Dimensions
VideoWave will stretch a smaller image and add a black background to fill the video screen. A way to avoid this is to copy and paste several smaller images on a new canvas of full screen size (720×480 for DVD).

Exporting PowerPoint Slides for DVD Productions

Start

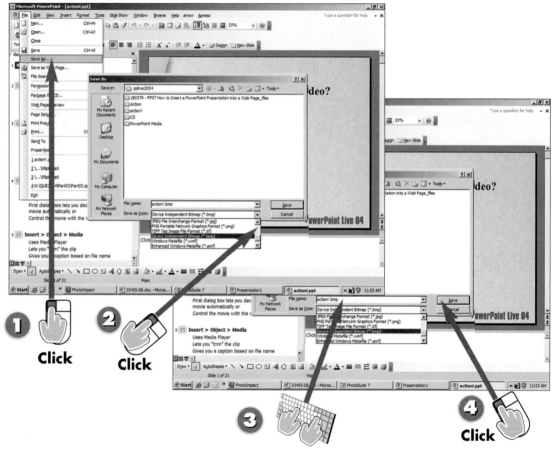

1 Click **File**, **Save As** in PowerPoint.

2 Click the drop-down menu to select **BMP**.

3 Type a name.

4 Click **Save**.

You can also export PowerPoint slides to use in DVD Slideshows, or as background menu images. Use this technique to add your PowerPoint slides to your DVD projects.

Using the BMP File Type
Selecting the standard Windows BMP file type will keep the images uncompressed and enable you to see the thumbnails in VideoWave or DVD Builder.

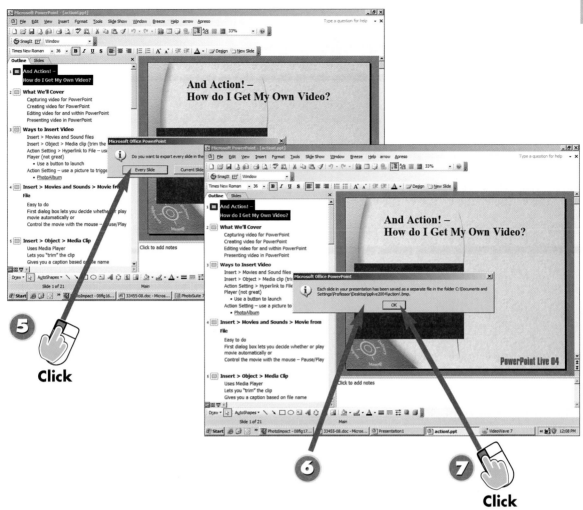

Click

(5) Click **Every Slide** to export all the slides in the file.

(6) Note the folder where the files are saved.

(7) Click **OK**.

See next page

Creating the Slide Show
With the slides exported as images to a folder you designate, you can use the techniques we learned in Part 5, "Creating a Slideshow from Images," to create a slide show in VideoWave's Storyline view.

Creating a New Destination Folder
You can also create a new destination folder for the slides before exporting (by right-clicking in another main folder), or create a New Folder directly in the Save As window with the **Create New Folder** button.

8

9 **Click**

[Screenshot of VideoWave 7 - Production 2 application window showing the Media Selector - Folders with slide thumbnails (Slide1.BMP through Slide21.BMP) and the Production Editor - Storyline with numbered slide frames 1 through 12]

8 Open the folder with the exported PowerPoint images as a VideoWave production.

9 Click **Storyline** to create a slide show.

With the slides exported to a folder, you are ready to create a slide show from the content in VideoWave. While you could add the slides to a Collection, it's just as easy at this point to access them all at once from their file folder.

Preview the Slide Show
Before creating a final movie of the slide show, check the duration of the slides and any transitions you may add by playing the production in the Preview Window.

Click

10

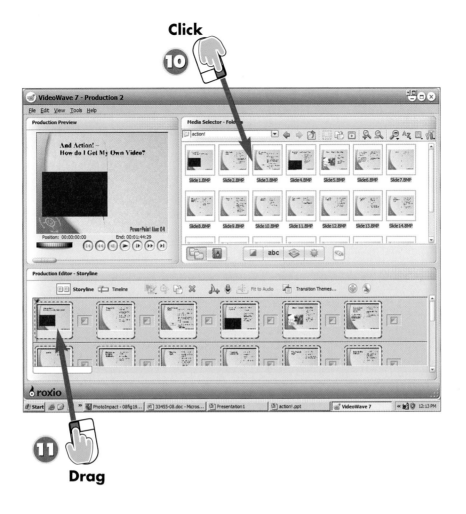

11

Drag

10 Select the images you want as slides.

11 Drag them into the Storyline to create a Slideshow.

End

Putting Slides in Order
Use the File View drop-down arrow menu in the Folder view to re-sort the slides. Click **View**, **Details** and then click on **Name** to sort by the file name and sequential number.

Exporting One Slide
If you want just one slide to use for a menu background or a single title in the DVD, just click to save only the **Current Slide** in step 5.

Capturing Music from LPs or Cassettes

Start

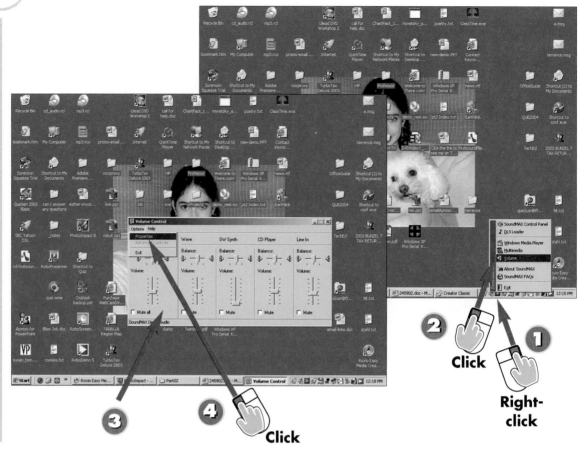

1. Right-click the **Sound** icon in your System Tray

2. Click to select **Volume**.

3. Note that you can set the levels for Playback of all of your audio devices connected to your sound card.

4. Click **Options**, **Properties** to open up Recording Properties.

INTRODUCTION

Previously, we used the Roxio Capture Component to capture video from a DV camcorder and images from a scanner and digital camera. Now we will use it to capture music from older sources like LPs or cassettes (also known as *analog audio*). But first, this task walks you through opening your Recording Options to make sure that the Line In source of your sound card is active.

TIP

This first set of options is only for Playback. It will affect only the sound that normally comes out of your PC. We need to get to the stuff that is going into the computer, which is why we're digging a whole lot deeper.

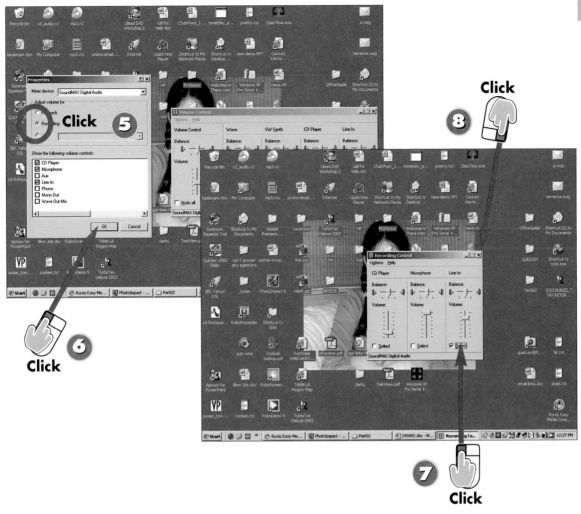

5 Click **Recording** to access the recording options.

6 Click **OK**.

7 Click to set **Line In** as the recording device (not Microphone or CD player).

8 Click the X in the upper-right corner to close the dialog box.

See next page

Setting the Input Level
First drag the sliders to make the incoming sound as true as possible. Then, if your final result's volume is too low, you may need to drag the incoming level slider higher. On the other hand, if you get too much noise or distortion, try dragging it lower.

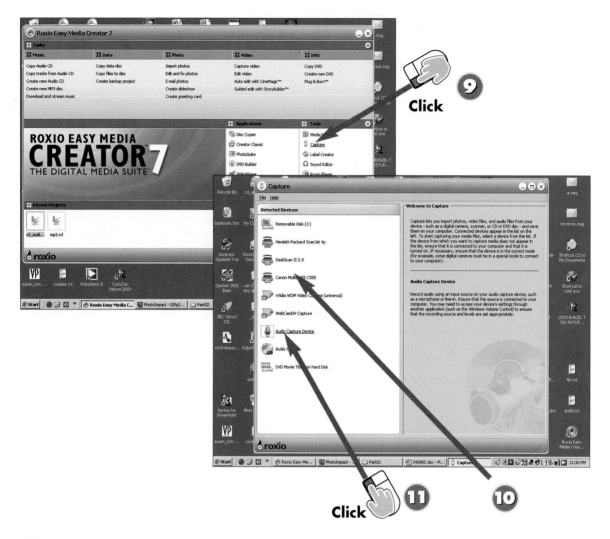

Click ⑨

Click ⑪ ⑩

⑨ Open Roxio and on the Start Page, click **Capture**.

⑩ Hover your mouse over any of the devices to learn more about them (and review steps for setup).

⑪ Click **Audio Capture Device**.

INTRODUCTION

Now we're ready to use the Roxio Capture Window to grab analog audio. Remember that we originally used it in Part 4, "Acquiring Still Images," **p.116**. It's like the Swiss Army Knife of acquiring digital media from all kinds of sources, including analog audio.

TIP

Seeing Your Peripherals in Capture
Some capture devices in your system will require device drivers and software to enable them. Others may not appear unless they are actively turned on or in use. Check the manual for these devices and make sure you follow instructions and load the appropriate programs from any installation CD or DVD.

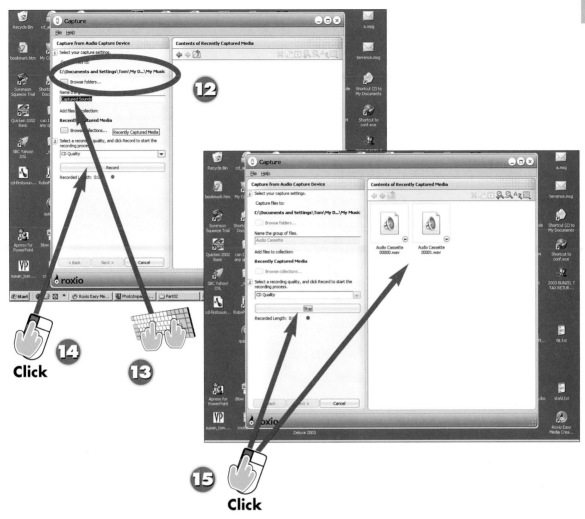

Click 14   13

Click 15

12 Note the destination folder on your hard drive where the captured files will go.

13 Type in a new name for your audio.

14 Click **Record** to begin recording the incoming sound.

15 Click **Stop** to end the recording. Your recorded segments are added to your collections in Capture (and become digital files in the destination folder).

End

Seeing Capture in Progress
When audio is recorded the red light in Capture will blink on and off. Clicking the little arrow in the corner of the icon representing the captured files will play them back (temporarily replacing the incoming audio).

Check the Default Capture Folder
To check (or change) the default destination folder for the files you capture in the Capture utility, click **File**, **Options**.

Recording into Sound Editor

Start

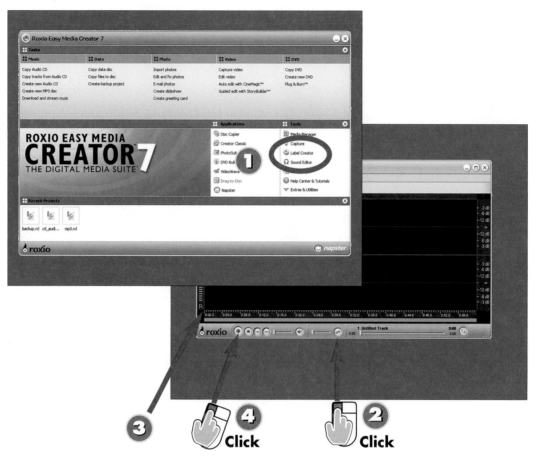

3   4 **Click**   2 **Click**

1   Open **Sound Editor** from the Roxio Start Page.

2   Click the **microphone** button.

3   You should see the levels of incoming audio. Notice that the Play/Pause button has become a red Recording button.

4   Click **Record** to begin recording. The Record button turns into a Pause button.

A more powerful tool used for editing your sound files in Easy Media Creator is the Sound Editor. As we'll see here, you can use the Sound Editor to select, modify, and save portions of a captured audio segment. If you want to create your own audio files for your projects, this is a tool to learn more about.

You're Still Using Line-In

Even though the button is shown as a Microphone, if Line In is enabled in your sound card, you can use Line In for better audio quality. You should only use the microphone if you have no Line In option available because the sound from a microphone is much quieter, so it needs a special jack to compensate. Generally Line In is higher fidelity (stereo) while the microphone is more limited in range (mono).

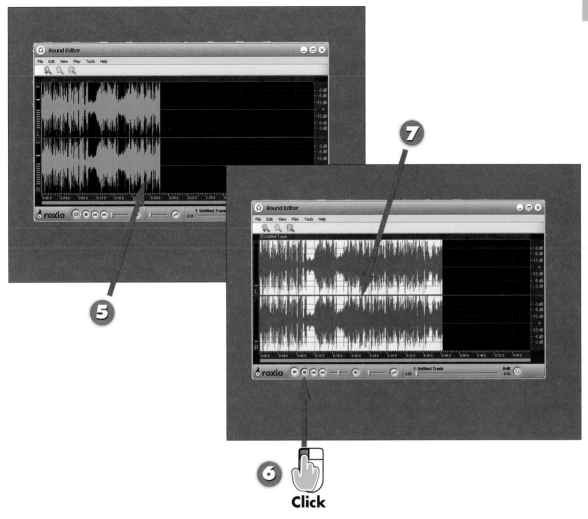

Click

5 Watch the incoming audio enter the timeline.

6 Click **Stop** to end recording. You will hear the incoming audio continue although it is no longer being recorded.

7 The captured audio segment is highlighted in the editor.

See next page

Troubleshooting Audio Levels
If you don't see incoming audio levels, check Recording Device and Recording Source in the **Tools** column of the Main Menu.

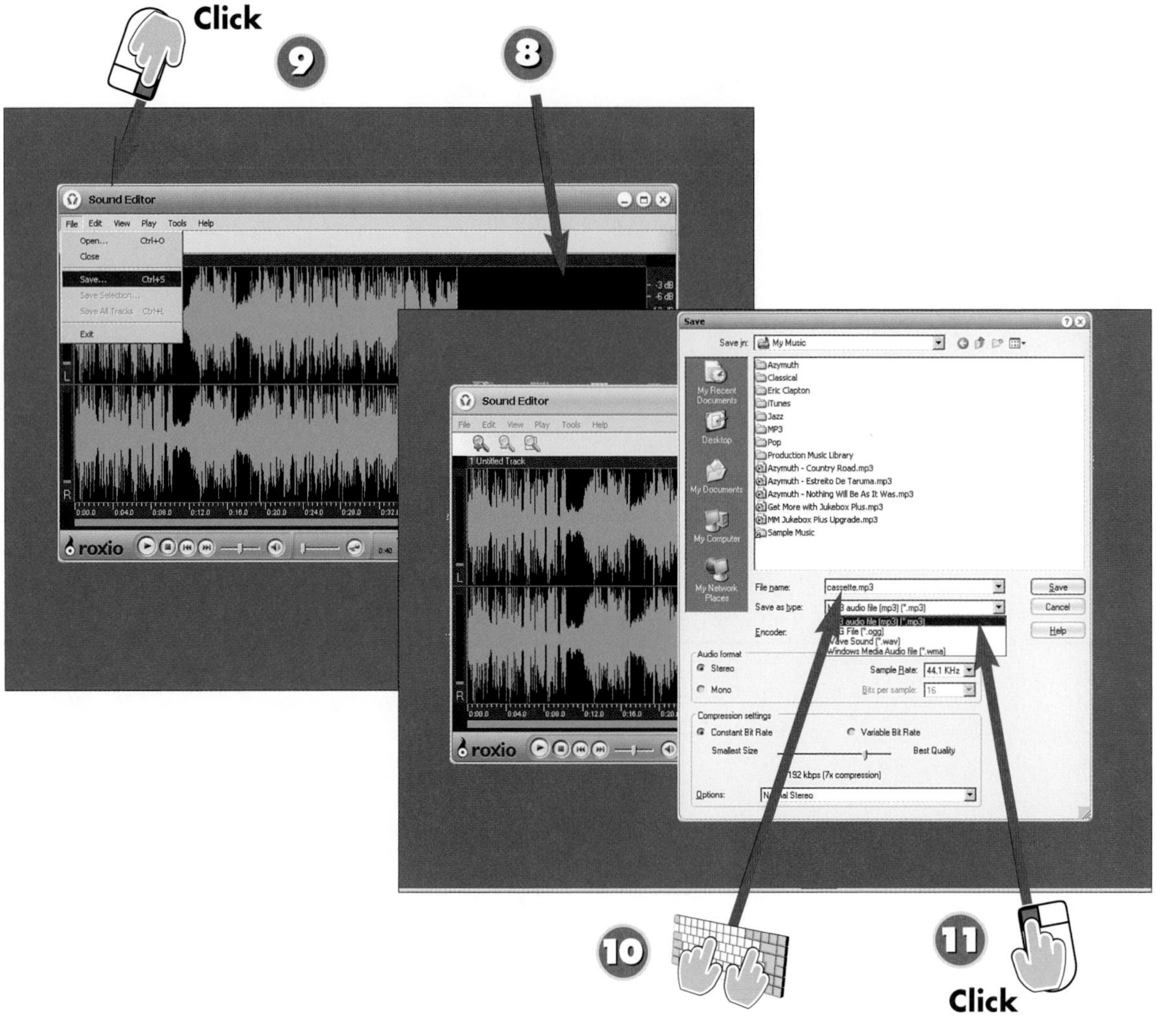

Click

9 **8**

10 **11**

Click

8 Click outside the highlighted (captured) segment to deselect it.

9 Click **File**, **Save** from the main menu.

10 Name your file something appropriate, like **Cassette**.

11 Click to select the output file type (WAV for a DVD project).

Now that we've brought our audio into Sound Editor, we'll begin to see its superior options for manipulating and saving our final file in the format we may need for different purposes.

Choosing a File Type
Selecting **MP3** will give you an active quality slider. Choosing **WAV** will set the audio quality at the highest (CD Quality) level by default, but you can select a *lower sampling rate*.

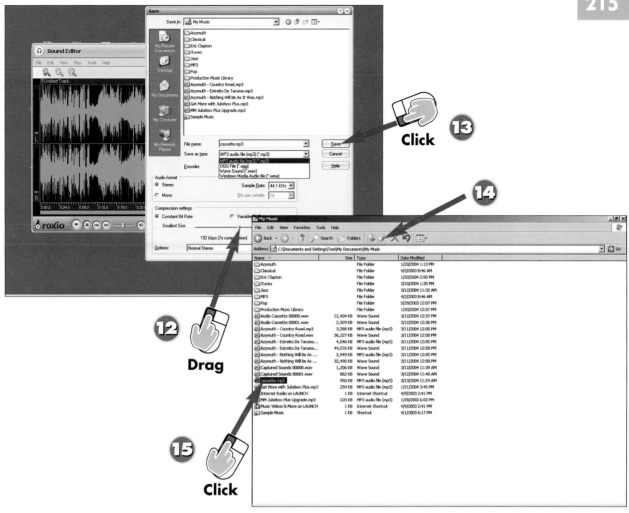

Drag

Click

12 If MP3 is selected, select a quality setting by dragging the slider. You will need to try different settings to see what your taste finds acceptable.

13 Click **Save**.

14 Open the designated folder for saved music (such as My Music in My Documents).

15 Listen and compare your recorded file with other music you have ripped, downloaded, or captured.

End

The Capture Utility
The Capture Utility (discussed earlier in "Capturing Music from LPs or Cassettes") is good for quick and dirty grabbing of songs from analog sources, and gives you a quick project or collections view of captured segments. It does not allow editing.

Why Use the Sound Editor?
The Sound Editor is more sophisticated than the Capture utility and lets you edit and save *selected* portions of an audio track. If you explore the output options, you can also fine tune your settings for MP3 quality and use different MP3 audio encoders.

Applying an Effect to the Whole Song (Normalize)

Start

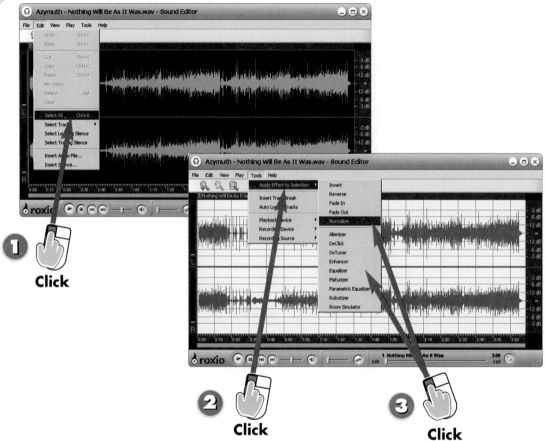

1 Click

2 Click

3 Click

1 Click **Edit**, **Select All** on the main menu (or press Ctrl+A).

2 Choose **Tools**, **Apply Effect to Transition**.

3 Look over the list of Effects. Click **Normalize**.

INTRODUCTION

Some effects that you would apply will probably work best over the entire track. For example, you might want to use *Normalize* to level the volume peaks. You can apply any Sound Editor effect easily over an entire track.

HINT

When to Normalize
This effect is useful when you have recorded multiple tracks that may have been originally recorded at various volume levels, for example on a "mix" cassette.

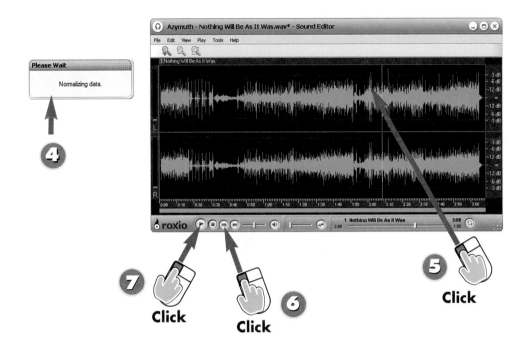

Click

Click

Click

Click

4) Depending on the length of the track, Normalize takes a little while. You will see slight changes in the levels of the track.

5) Click elsewhere to deselect the track.

6) Click to go to the beginning of the track.

7) Click to **Play** the track to see if it sounds okay.

End

TIP

Saving the Track
If you click **Save**, the track with the applied effect (Normalize) replaces your original. To be safe, click to select all again and choose **File**, **Save Selection** to give your version a new name and location.

Enhancing and Equalizing

Start

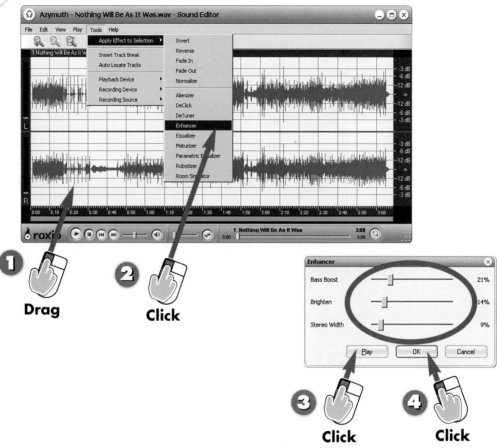

Drag

Click

Click

Click

1. Select all or part of the track by clicking and dragging through it, or using **Ctrl+A** to select all.

2. Click **Tools**, **Add Effect to Selection**, **Enhancer**.

3. Drag the sliders to change the settings. Click **Play** to hear how it sounds.

4. Click **OK** to implement the changes to the selected part of the track. (It will take a few seconds to render.)

There are other fun ways to change the sounds within a portion or for the entire track. You can also alter the bass, brighten (similar to treble), and modify the distance between the stereo speakers. It's like having your own sound studio on the desktop.

TIP

Don't Click Save
Don't save the effect version of a track over a version you've ripped or downloaded unless you're sure you like the results. Choose **File**, **Save Selection** and give it a new name and/or a new location (Effect Versions).

HINT

Trial and Error
It is hard to know how these kind of special effects will sound before you try them out. Until you've worked with them for a while, trial and error will be the only way to get the results you want.

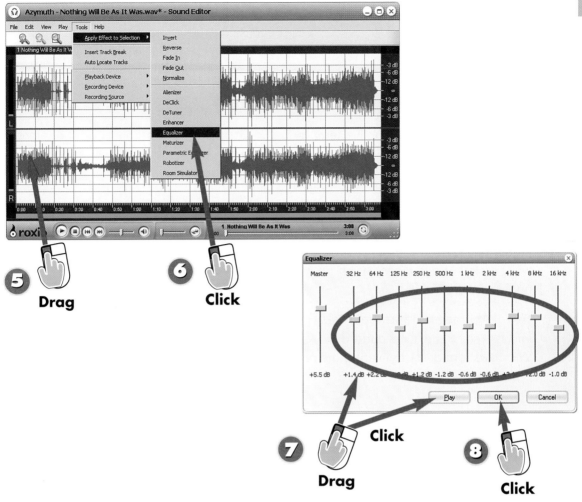

5 Select all or part of the track by dragging through it, or using **Ctrl+A** to select all.

6 Click **Tools**, **Add Effect to Selection**, **Equalizer**.

7 Drag the sliders to change the settings. Click **Play** to hear how it sounds.

8 Click **OK** to implement the changes to the selected part of the track. (It will take a few seconds to render.)

End

Right-Click for Effects
Another way to open the effects list is to right-click on the selection area.

Maturizer
An effect to try is the Maturizer, which combines several of the other effects, like the Enhancer, Equalizer, and DeClick.

Glossary

A

Audio   An alternative term for sound.

Audio Level   An alternative term for audio volume.

Audio Track   One of several individual songs or compositions on an audio CD or tape.

AutoPlaylist   The order in which files will be played automatically on an MP3 audio disc.

AVI   Abbreviation for *Audio Video Interleaved*, this is the standard Windows format for delivering uncompressed video.

B

Bit   Short for *binary digit*, this is the smallest unit of data recognized by a PC.

Bit Rate   The number of bits transferred per second.

Button   An icon on the DVD Menu that when clicked takes the user to another location on the disc (see also **DVD Menu**).

C

Capture   Recording audio, video, or still images as digital information in a movie project file.

Capture Device   Hardware used in transferring audio and video from an external source, such as a camcorder or VCR, to a computer.

CD   Stands for "Compact Disc," the standard digital medium for audio and data.

Chapter   A portion of a DVD movie "Title" (or longer track) referenced for easy access by a thumbnail in a menu.

Clip   A segment of a video extracted from a larger video file.

Codec   Software or hardware used to compress and decompress digital media.

Collection   A file container within Roxio Easy Media Creator used to organize video clips, images, and audio.

Color Panel   A selector of swatches from which to choose a color for a background, text, or other element.

Compression   The process of reducing a file size by removing redundant information from the file.

Creator Classic   The CD and DVD burning component or Roxio Easy Media Creator.

Crossfade   A video transition method where the frames in the current clip fade out as frames in the new clip fade in.

D

Digital8   Sony's proprietary digital video format, which is backward compatible with Hi8. This format uses standard 8mm tape to record and store video data.

Digital Artifacts   Distorted areas in a video or image file, often appearing as square shapes within the picture.

Digital Camcorder   A device for recording video in a digital format. Common digital camcorders capture video in mini-DV, Digital8, and DVD MPEG-2 formats.

Digital Video (DV)   Video and sound stored in a digital format.

Dual Layer   A new format of DVD disc that can hold twice the amount of data as the more traditional single layer media.

Duration   A set interval of time to display content, usually for a still image slide or transition effect.

DV Peripheral   A device used to move DV video from a camcorder or other source to the computer's hard drive during capture.

DV-AVI   An uncompressed Microsoft audio/video format used to encode camcorder data into a format usable by video editing programs.

DVD   A digital medium or disc used to store and distribute data or movies, usually containing 4.7 gigabytes of space.

DVD Builder   The component of Roxio Easy Media Creator that lets the user organize and burn a DVD comprised of titles and chapters.

DVD Menu   The interface on some DVD discs that allows the user to navigate through its content and choose which movies, titles, or chapters to view.

E–F

Easy Media Creator   A suite of programs from the company (Roxio) enabling the user to manipulate images, sounds, and movies.

Effect(s)   A special effect applied to video footage in VideoWave or DVD Builder.

End Point   The position or marker on a video clip where it is trimmed to eliminate footage after that point in time.

Fade   A transitional effect designed to bring the video from or to black by gradually decreasing or increasing light in the picture.

File Reference   A way to indicate the location or use of another computer file.

FireWire   A high-speed data serial transfer standard providing connectivity for a wide range of devices, including camcorders, external hard drives, and portable media devices. (See also *IEEE 1394* and *i.LINK*.)

Frame   One single image in the series of images making up a video.

Frame Rate   The number of video frames displayed per second. Most DV camcorders record video at 29.97 frames per second. In general, the higher the frame rate the smoother the picture.

G-J

IEEE 1394   A high-speed data serial transfer standard providing connectivity for a wide range of devices, including camcorders, external hard drives, and portable media devices. (See also *FireWire* and *i.LINK*.)

i.LINK   The Sony implementation of IEEE 1394. (See also *FireWire* and *IEEE 1394*.)

Internet Radio   Radio stations that can be accessed through a web browser.

K-M

Keyframe(able)   The portion of a video clip that can be accessed by a reference marker or chapter because it is uncompressed. Also, a marker or point of a clip in which something changes, so that animation can be applied.

Line Noise   Unwanted noise in an audio track caused by electrical currents interfering with the transmission of audio data through a cable.

Marker   An indicator on a clip of something to be noted, such as an End Point.

Microphone Noise   Unwanted sound captured when a microphone is bumped during recording.

Mini-DV   The format common to most digital video camcorders, which uses 6.35mm tape to record and store video data.

MP3   Compressed music file format popular on the Web for downloads and among audiophiles for storage.

MP3 Player   Portable device used to transport and enjoy compressed music files.

MPG   Compressed video file format (stands for *Motion Pictures Experts Group*).

MPEG-1   Standard quality MPG video file (VHS quality) used on VCD discs.

MPEG-2   High quality MPG video file used on DVD discs.

N-R

Nero   Name for the suite of programs from the company Ahead used to extract and burn digital media and images.

Nero Burning ROM   Program from the company Ahead primarily used to extract and burn digital media and images.

Nero Express   Component of the Nero suite of programs that can be used to burn audio, video, and data CDs and DVDs with a minimum number of options or steps.

NTSC   National Television Standards Committee. This is most commonly referenced in terms of the technical standard for video formatting in the United States.

Overlay   An additional layer of content on top of another in a video clip or graphic composition.

PAL   Phase Alternative Line. A competing standards body to NTSC. Most of the world outside the U.S. conforms to video standards based on PAL.

PhotoSuite   The component in Easy Media Creator used to manipulate still images.

Playlist   The order in which items will play on a compact disc.

Plug-in   A software program that enables another program (particularly a web browser) to perform a certain function.

Preview   The feature of a program, generally for video, to see how a final production will look before it is saved or rendered.

Project (or Project File)   The master file used by Roxio and other programs to store information about imported data and how it is arranged within the project.

-R(W)   Stands for "minus R"; a specific recordable DVD media format. "W" means rewritable.

+R(W)   Stands for "plus R"; specific recordable DVD media format. "W" means rewritable.

S

Source   Device containing audio and video content to be captured and encoded by video-editing programs.

Split   Dividing one larger audio or video clip into two smaller clips.

Storyboard   A program in Easy Media Creator similar to VideoWave that enables the production of slide shows composed of still images.

Storyline   A view in Easy Media Creator's VideoWave that breaks up a production into chunks of content for easier editing (as opposed to the Timeline). Very similar to Storyboard.

Super 8   A film format introduced by Kodak in 1965, which uses 8mm cartridge-loaded film reels for recording movies.

S-Video   Sometimes referred to as S-VHS, this video transmission format separates black-and-white video information from color data into two signals. Traditional composite video sends this information as one signal.

T–V

Tags   Indicators saved with MP3 songs that let the user locate them on a peripheral device by artist, track, and so on. (See also *Playlist*.)

Timeline   A detailed workspace view of a VideoWave project showing relative lengths of each element used within the project and how they overlap.

Transition   A special kind of effect placed between two movie clips or images to smooth the change to the next scene.

Trim   Hiding parts of an audio or video clip in the project space without permanently removing them from the source file. Audio and video clips can be trimmed by adjusting the start or end trim points, which alters playback within the project, while leaving the original file intact.

Trim Points   Markers on the timeline of a project file designating the starting and ending points for a particular media clip.

Video   A succession of rapidly moving images (frames per second) that simulate movement.

Video Track   One component of a video composition in a video editor than is used to create a final (rendered) production.

VideoWave   The video editing component of Roxio Easy Media Creator.

W-Z

WAV   Standard Windows audio file type.

Windows Media Player   The Windows program used to play music and video files, and also to access online digital content.

Windows Media file   A file containing audio, video, or script data stored in Windows Media Format. Depending on content and purpose, Windows Media files use a variety of filename extensions, including .wma, .wme, .wms, .wmv, .wmx, .wmz, or .wvx.

Wizard   A specialized series of menus or dialog boxes that enable the user to accomplish a specific tasks by breaking down the objective into a series of predefined choices.

WMA   Standard Windows audio file type used mainly for compressed web content.

WMV   Standard Windows video file type used mainly for compressed web content.

Workspace   The area of VideoWave where movies, audio, or images (slide shows) are pieced together. The workspace is made up of two views: Storyline and Timeline.

Zoom   Magnifying or shrinking the image viewed by a camera lens, making the object appear closer or farther than it actually is in physical space.

E - F

P